OSPREY COMBAT AIRCRAFT • 27

AIR WAR IN THE GULF 1991

SERIES EDITOR: TONY HOLMES

OSPREY COMBAT AIRCRAFT • 27

AIR WAR IN THE GULF 1991

CHRISTOPHER CHANT

OSPREY
PUBLISHING

Front cover
The UN forces' 18th kill of the Gulf War came on 26 January 1991 when a McDonnell Douglas F-15C Eagle (85-0104 of the 58th TFS/33rd TFW), flown by Captain Anthony F. Schiavi of the USAF, was the launch platform for an AIM-7 Sparrow medium range missile that brought down a Mikoyan-Gurevich MiG-23

First published in Great Britain in 2001 by Osprey Publishing
Elms Court, Chapel Way, Botley, Oxford, OX2 9LP
Email: info@ospreypublishing.com

© 2001 Osprey Publishing

ISBN 1 84176 295 4

Page design by TT Designs, T & B Truscott
Index by Alan Thatcher
Cover Artwork by Iain Wyllie
Aircraft Profiles and Scale Drawings by Mark Styling

Origination by Grasmere Digital Imaging, Leeds, UK
Printed through Bookbuilders, Hong Kong

01 02 03 04 05   10 9 8 7 6 5 4 3 2 1

For a catalogue of all Osprey Publishing titles please contact us at:

Osprey Direct UK, PO Box 140, Wellingborough, Northants NN8 4ZA, UK
E-mail: info@ospreydirect.co.uk

Osprey Direct USA, c/o Motorbooks International, 729 Prospect Ave,
PO Box 1, Osceola, WI 54020, USA
E-mail: info@ospreydirectusa.com

Or visit our website: www.ospreypublishing.com

CONTENTS

OCCUPATION OF KUWAIT

In 1961 the United Kingdom granted formal independence to the protectorate of Kuwait, which then became the Emirate of Kuwait. This small but oil-rich nation had long been coveted by Iraq, its much larger northern neighbour, which had become completely independent of the UK's League of Nations (and later United Nations) mandate in 1958, the year in which its monarchy was overthrown by the Ba'athist republic. Iraq never recognised Kuwait, and on several occasions in the following 30 years laid claim to all or part of it. Apart from its large oil reserves, reckoned in 1995 at 96.5 billion barrels to Iraq's 100 billion barrels, Iraq wanted Kuwait for its comparatively extensive coast along the western side of the Persian Gulf's northern end, as Iraq only has a very short coast, within military reach of Iran. Iraq followed mainly the Sunni branch of Islam and had a strong antipathy to Iran and its adherence to the Shi'a branch of Islam. Coupled with the desire to seize the oil-rich regions along Iran's western border, this was sufficient to persuade the Iraqi dictator, Saddam Hussein, to launch a major war against Iran in 1980. This conflict, which was very costly in terms of casualties and money, lasted until 1988 without any real resolution.

At the end of the war Iraq was crippled by debts, and saw in the seizure of Kuwait a chance to refill her coffers, rebuild her prestige among the Arab nations and satisfy her long-held claim to the country. After a short diplomatic offensive designed to justify her imminent action by claims of Kuwaiti encroachment on Iraqi oil reserves and Kuwaiti efforts to keep down the price of oil as a form of direct aggression against Iraq, Iraqi forces moved into Kuwait on 2 August 1990. Isolated pockets of Kuwaiti troops fought back but were unable to check the spearhead forces of the Iraqi Republican Guard, and by the end of the day the Iraqis were in control of virtually all of Kuwait. The Kuwaiti royal family and large numbers of Kuwaitis fled to neighbouring Saudi Arabia.

By the end of 2 August the United Nations Security Council had passed Resolution 660 demanding immediate withdrawal of the Iraqi occupation forces and the start of negotiations to end the dispute

In 1990 the air forces of the Persian Gulf region were equipped with a moderately large number of advanced aircraft, mostly of Western origin. The largest of these forces was the Royal Saudi Air Force, which operated from modern and well equipped bases with aircraft such as the Panavia Tornado IDS (foreground) and McDonnell Douglas F-15C Eagle (background), here flanking a SEPECAT Jaguar of the Sultan of Oman's Air Force *(RSAF)*

GULF STATES AND MAIN AIR BASES

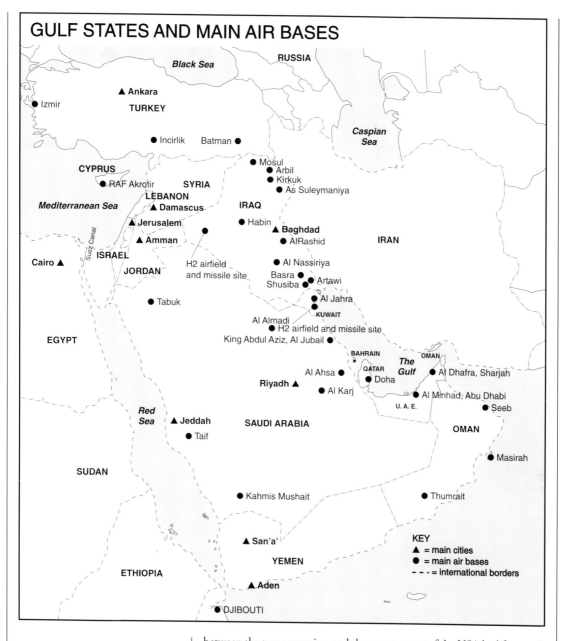

RUSSIA

Black Sea

▲ Ankara

● Izmir

TURKEY

Caspian Sea

● Incirlik   Batman ●

CYPRUS

● Mosul
● Arbil
● Kirkuk
● As Suleymaniya

● RAF Akrotir   SYRIA

LEBANON

Mediterranean Sea   ▲ Damascus   IRAQ

▲ Jerusalem   ● Habin

●   ▲ Baghdad   IRAN
● AlRashid

▲ Amman

Cairo ▲   ISRAEL

JORDAN   ● Al Nassiriya

H2 airfield   Basra ●
and missile site   Shusiba ● ● Artawi

● Tabuk   ● Al Jahra

KUWAIT

Al Almadi
● H2 airfield and missile site
King Abdul Aziz, Al Jubail ●

EGYPT   BAHRAIN   OMAN
The
Al Ahsa ●   QATAR   Gulf   ● Al Dhafra, Sharjah
● Doha
Riyadh ▲   ● Al Minhad, Abu Dhabi
● Al Karj   U. A. E.   ● Seeb

Red Sea   ▲ Jeddah   OMAN
● Taif
SAUDI ARABIA

● Masirah

SUDAN

● Kahmis Mushait   ● Thumrait

KEY
▲ San'a'   ▲ = main cities
● = main air bases
YEMEN   - - - = international borders

ETHIOPIA

▲ Aden

● DJIBOUTI

between the two countries, and the government of the USA had frozen all Iraqi and Kuwaiti assets. On 6 August King Fahd of Saudi Arabia asked for foreign military aid to defend his kingdom against the possibility of further Iraqi aggression, and Resolution 661 was passed to place a trade embargo on Iraq. In occupied Kuwait, Iraqi forces began to seize the nationals of Western nations, and in Iraq Saddam said that Iraq's tenure of Kuwait was 'irreversible'. In the USA President George Bush ordered the immediate planning for Operation 'Desert Shield', which would mean the rapid despatch of large American forces to the region, starting with the air transport to Saudi Arabia of the US Army's 82nd Airborne Division.

In a move to secure his eastern flank, Saddam then ordered that all Iraqi troops pull out of any Iranian territory still occupied after the 1980-88 Gulf

War, and that all Iranian prisoners-of-war be repatriated. The Western hostages were released on 28 August and by early December all remaining foreign nationals were allowed to leave Iraq and Kuwait, ending the possibility of 'human shields' being used to protect vital Iraqi targets.

The succession of events from this point to the increasingly inevitable outbreak of hostilities between Iraq and the coalition of forces created to free Kuwait from Iraqi occupation is most succinctly treated in diary form.

6 August 1990: The UN orders economic sanctions and a trade embargo on Iraq.

7 August: Some 48 McDonnell Douglas F-15C/D Eagle multi-role fighters of the US Air Force's 1st Tactical Fighter Wing (TFW) fly non-stop from Langley Air Force Base (AFB), Virginia, to Dhahran in Saudi Arabia in history's longest operational fighter deployment, lasting between 14 and 17 hours and including six or seven inflight refuellings. In subsequent days more than 20 more squadrons of US aircraft fly direct from US and European bases to Saudi Arabia.

8 August: The Iraqi government annexes Kuwait as Iraq's 19th province. President George Bush announces that 'a line has been drawn in the sand' and that 60,000 US troops may be sent to Saudi Arabia. The UK government reveals its plan to despatch naval and air force units to the Persian Gulf. The aircraft carrier USS *Dwight D. Eisenhower* and her battle group arrive in the Red Sea. USAF Boeing B-52 Stratofortress heavy bombers begin a deployment to the base on Diego Garcia island in the Indian Ocean.

9 August: The UN Security Council passes Resolution 662 declaring Iraq's annexation of Kuwait null and void. The British government announces

Seen with the fuselage legend 'Free Kuwait', this is one of the McDonnell Douglas A-4KU aircraft which escaped from Kuwait at the time of the Iraqi occupation to serve alongside the coalition air forces. It was based on the A-4M Skyhawk II of the US Marine Corps with additional electronic equipment carried in the fuselage 'hump' (Ian Black)

The great range of the Grumman F-14A Tomcat air-superiority fighter allowed the type to operate over Iraq from aircraft carriers deployed in the Red Sea. This is a machine of the VF-32 'Swordsmen' squadron, part of CVW-3 (Carrier Wing-3) operating from the USS *John F. Kennedy* (Lt Cdr Parsons, USN)

One of four HARM-carrying F-4G 'Wild Weasel' aircraft is seen taking on fuel from a Boeing KC-135R Stratotanker, one of the two primary types of tanker aircraft operated by the US Air Force for the support of strategic as well as tactical aircraft in the air campaign against Iraq *(DoD via Robert F Dorr)*

that the first stage in Operation 'Granby', the build-up of British forces in the region, is the despatch of one Panavia Tornado F 3 fighter squadron and one SEPECAT Jaguar attack squadron to the Persian Gulf.

10 August: Saddam demands that Moslems all over the world join Iraq's 'jihad' (holy war) against the USA and Israel in the event that any effort is made to drive the Iraqi forces from Kuwait. One squadron of the Royal Air Force's Tornado F 3 force arrives at Dhahran.

11 August: The first 500 Egyptian troops arrive in Saudi Arabia. One squadron of RAF Jaguars lands at Thumrait in Oman.

12 August: Saddam starts his 'peace initiative', offering to consider an end to the occupation of Kuwait if Israel and Syria terminate their occupation of territories in Palestine and Lebanon. Dismissed peremptorily by the members of the growing coalition, this offer is often repeated in the following months. The F-15E strike/attack aircraft of the 4th TFW start to move to Saudi Arabia from Seymour Johnson AFB. Three of the RAF's BAe Nimrod maritime patrol aircraft land at Seeb in Oman as a boost to naval units blockading Iraq's seaborne trade.

13 August: In Operation 'Salamandre', the French aircraft carrier *Clemenceau* departs for Djibouti on the Red Sea with 42 anti-tank helicopters of the French Force d'Action Rapide. Belgium and the Netherlands also signal their decision to send naval forces to the region.

15 August: In a move to secure his eastern flank, Saddam orders that all Iraqi troops pull out of any Iranian territory still occupied after the 1980-88 Gulf War, and that all Iranian prisoners-of-war still held in Iraq be repatriated. The US Navy's aircraft carrier USS *John F. Kennedy* and her battle group depart Norfolk, Virginia, to become a major element of the American forces mustering in and round Saudi Arabia for 'Desert Shield'.

17 August: Saddam announces that seized Western nationals, including women and children, are being located at possible targets of coalition air attacks as 'human shields'. The build-up of American forces in Saudi Arabia forges ahead, however, with an average of about 120 strategic transport aircraft sorties arriving each day.

18 August: The UN Security Council passes Resolution 664 demanding that Iraq frees all foreign nationals in Iraq and Kuwait, and rescinds its closure of foreign diplomatic missions in Kuwait.

21 August: The first of 22 Lockheed F-117A Night Hawk 'stealth' attack aircraft of the USAF's 415th Tactical Fighter Squadron (TFS), 37th TFW, land in Saudi Arabia.

23 August: Dick Cheney, the American Secretary of Defense, calls the first Reserve and National Guard forces to active duty, beginning with three Lockheed C-141B StarLifter and two Lockheed C-5A Galaxy strategic transport squadrons.

24 August: Iraqi troops surround embassies in Kuwait that have refused to close.

25 August: The UN Security Council passes Resolution 665, providing a legal framework for members of the coalition to employ limited force in compelling compliance with the trade sanctions on Iraq and Kuwait. By this date the US Navy's aircraft carrier USS *Saratoga* (replacing the *Dwight D. Eisenhower)* and the battleship USS *Wisconsin,* together with their supporting vessels, have sailed into the Red Sea.

26 August: In a strange reversal of allegiances that would have been unimaginable only one year earlier, an RAF Nimrod maritime patrol aeroplane provides assistance to a Soviet navy warship in the interception of a suspected Iraqi blockade runner.

28 August: Saddam agrees to release foreign women and children held against their will in Iraq and Kuwait. The first squadron of RAF Tornado GR 1 interdictors lands in Saudi Arabia.

29 August: In the first aeroplane loss of 'Desert Shield', a C-5A Galaxy transport bound for Saudi Arabia with stores crashes on take-off from Ramstein AFB, Germany.

10 September: President George Bush of the USA and President Mikhail

With drop tanks, electronic warfare pods and two AIM-9 Sidewinder AAMs under its wing, this Tornado GR 1 carried a trio of 454 kg (1,000 lb) 'Paveway' laser-guided bombs under its fuselage. The aircraft lacked any organic laser-designation capability, illumination of the target being entrusted to a third party such as a BAe Buccaneer S 2B or another Tornado carrying one of the two available TIALD pods

Gorbachev of the CIS meet at Helsinki in Finland to co-ordinate measures to be taken against Iraq if Saddam refuses to pull his forces out of Kuwait.

13 September: The UK announces that 7th Armoured Brigade is to be redeployed from Germany to Saudi Arabia. By now the coalition air force units assembled in Saudi Arabia and her neighbours muster more combat aircraft than the Iraqi air force.

14 September: In Operation 'Locusta', Italy announces it will send a squadron of Tornado IDS attack aircraft to Abu Dhabi. Four USAF Reserve C-141B StarLifter squadrons are called to active duty.

15 September: France announces the imminent despatch of 4,000 troops to Saudi Arabia.

16 September: The UN Security Council passes Resolution 670 banning all air transport, with the exception of humanitarian flights, to and from airports in Iraq and Kuwait. The US Navy's carrier USS *Midway* sails from her home port at Yokosuka, Japan, for the Persian Gulf area at about this time.

21 September: Saddam's Revolutionary Command Council announces there is 'not a single chance of any retreat' from Kuwait, and that any effort to drive the Iraqi forces from that country will pave the way for 'the mother of all battles'.

25 September: The UN orders an air blockade of Iraq.

7 October: In Operation 'Scimitar', 12 McDonnell Douglas CF-18 Hornet fighters of the Canadian Armed Forces' No 409 Squadron move from Germany to Qatar.

8 October: The pace of training operations in the Persian Gulf region takes its toll as a McDonnell Douglas RF-4C Phantom II reconnaissance aeroplane of the Alabama Air National Guard (ANG) crashes near Abu Dhabi, with the death of both men on board; and two Bell UH-1N 'Huey' helicopters of the US Marine Corps crash in the northern part of the Arabian Sea, killing all eight personnel.

10 October: A General Dynamics F-111F 'Aardvark' interdictor of the USAF's 48th TFW crashes in the

During the 'Desert Shield' build-up, the USA committed some 1,700 helicopters to Saudi Arabia. Seen here on a length of disused runway serving as an interim landing strip are three US Marine Corps helicopters: two Bell AH-1W SuperCobra close support and one Bell UH-1N utility *(DoD via Robert F Dorr)*

Saudi Arabian desert, killing both crew members. As a result of this and other accidents, the USAF halts all 'Desert Shield' flying in Saudi Arabia (except for standing patrols by E-3 AWACS aircraft) pending a flight safety review. Flying restarts a few days later, and the accident rate is considerably lower from then on.

8 November: Saddam replaces the chief-of-staff of the Iraqi armed forces with Lieutenant General Hussein Rashid. President Bush announces that the US government plans to despatch a further 100,000 troops to Saudi Arabia. From this time to mid-January the strength of the USAF in the theatre doubles. Though not spelled out at the time, this signals the shift on the coalition's emphasis from the defence of Saudi Arabia to the expulsion of the Iraqi occupying forces from Kuwait. In this period allied Grumman F-14 Tomcat fighters of the US Navy join F-15s, F/A-18s and Tornados in high-speed probing flights toward Iraq, the aircraft turning back just short of the border. At the same time Boeing RC-135 electronic reconnaissance aircraft and E-3 AWACS machines keep a careful watch on Iraqi reactions (fighters and missiles, together with their associated radar equipment) gathering data vitally important to subsequent attacks. The Iraqi command later realises that the coalition forces are gathering information about Iraq's air-defence capability and orders its forces to ignore all such coalition probes.

19 November: Iraq reveals that it is allocating an additional 250,000 troops to the defence of its occupation of Kuwait.

22 November: The UK announces its intention of sending another 14,000 troops and more aircraft to Saudi Arabia.

28 November: Kuwaitis tell the UN that their country is now being ruthlessly plundered by Iraq.

29 November: By a majority of 12 to 2, the UN Security Council passes Resolution 678 authorising member states to use 'all necessary means' against Iraq, unless she pulls her forces out of Kuwait by 15 January 1991.

Men of one of the two US airborne divisions allocated to 'Desert Shield' arrive in Saudi Arabia on board a Lockheed C-5A Galaxy heavy transport of the 436th Military Airlift Wing of the US Air Force's Military Airlift Command

President Bush decides to send an additional 300 American aircraft to Saudi Arabia.

6 December: Saddam finally agrees to allow remaining foreign nationals to leave Iraq and Kuwait, which ends the possibility of 'human shields' being used to protect vital Iraqi targets.

13 December: The scale of the coalition's build-up in Saudi Arabia is shown by the US government's announcement of the presence in-theatre of 730 main battle tanks, 90 F-14 and F-15 air-superiority fighters, 335 Grumman A-6E Intruder, McDonnell Douglas/BAe AV-8B Harrier II, Fairchild Republic A-10A, F-111F and F-117A attack aircraft, and 220 F-15E, General Dynamics F-16 Fighting Falcon and F/A-18 Hornet dual-role aircraft, as well as support aircraft such as F-4G 'Wild Weasel' and EF-111A Raven electronic support aircraft, large numbers of McDonnell Douglas KC-10 and Boeing KC-135 Stratotankers, and several hundred helicopters and transport aircraft.

22 December: Iraq again says that she will never surrender Kuwait, and will use 'weapons of mass destruction' if attacked.

24 December: Saddam threatens that, in the event of hostilities, Iraq's first target will be Israel. This move was designed to provoke an Israeli reaction, and could have led to a split in the coalition if the Arab countries had refused to fight alongside Israel.

28 December: The US Navy's aircraft carriers USS *America* and *Theodore Roosevelt* depart the USA to bolster the American 'Desert Shield' forces.

2 January 1991: The North Atlantic Treaty Organisation announces it is to deploy 42 aircraft of the Allied Mobile Force to bases in southern Turkey to strengthen the defences of that area in the face of a possible diversionary attack by Saddam's forces in the north of Iraq. The force consists of 18 Dornier/Dassault AlphaJet A light attack aircraft from Germany, 18 Dassault Mirage 5 attack aircraft from Belgium and six Lockheed RF-104G Starfighter reconnaissance aircraft from Italy.

6 January: Saddam claims that the Iraqi forces are fully mobilised and at a high level of readiness to hold Iraq's position in Kuwait.

8 January: The USA reveals that there are 360,000 American personnel in the Persian Gulf region.

12 January: Congress votes to authorise President Bush to use force against Iraq in necessary.

15 January: The UN Security Council's deadline passes without any obvious sign of military action by the coalition forces.

THE IRAQI AIR FORCE

The coalition force gathered in and around Saudi Arabia believed their air forces would have first to defeat the Iraqi air force before their land forces could swing into action. In 1991 the Iraqi air force was generally thought to be the sixth largest in the world, comparatively well trained and equipped with substantial numbers of modern aircraft, largely of French and Soviet origins. However, there was surprisingly little in the way of concrete information on the disposition and exact strength of the Iraqi air force.

When the two sides came to blows in January 1991, the Iraqi air force mustered some 550 front-line aircraft in the fighter, attack, bomber and reconnaissance roles. Under the command of Lieutenant General Hamid Sha'abeen al Khazraji, the Iraqi air force had some 40,000 men, and its first-line assets were divided between the Air Defence Command and the Air Support Command.

The Air Defence Command's primary responsibility was the defence of the country's air bases and its targets of strategic significance. For this task the command controlled all of the air force's interceptor units, the air surveillance radars, and the control and reporting system through which radar data were turned into a cohesive air-defence scheme. The Air Defence command also controlled the various parts of the Iraqi army tasked with the protection of strategic targets with surface-to-air missiles and anti-aircraft artillery.

Up to a time one or two days before the outbreak of hostilities, the Air Defence Command had some three Adnan AWACS aircraft, which were Ilyushin Il-76 'Candid' transports locally adapted to carry French radar equipment, the Thomson-CSF Tigre. The real capability of these

Suppression of Iraq's large and potentially devastating collection of surface-to-air missiles and anti-aircraft artillery was a high priority for the coalition air forces. For the Americans, this all-important SEAD (Suppression of Enemy Air Defences) role was entrusted largely to the McDonnell Douglas F-4G 'Wild Weasel' version of the venerable Phantom II multi-role fighter. These two F-4Gs, operated by the 35th Tactical Fighter Wing home based at George Air Force Base in California, each carry four AGM-88A HARM (High-speed Anti-Radiation Missile) weapons *(DoD via David F Brown)*

Throughout Operation 'Desert Storm', members of the coalition forces were on a high state of alert for any Iraqi use of 'weapons of mass destruction'. These two pilots of a Fleet Air Arm Westland Sea King HC 4 helicopter are wearing NBC (Nuclear, Biological and Chemical) protection suits complete with electrically powered portable air filtration units *(DPR (N), Crown Copyright)*

technically important aircraft is still not known as they were not used in the air campaign over Iraq and Kuwait. One of them was badly damaged on the ground, and the other two flew to the physical safety of neutral Iran.

In overall terms, the Iraqi air force has never concerned itself greatly with the problems of differentiating friend from foe in confused tactical situations. In the Gulf War between Iraq and Iran, the Iraqi army created an anti-aircraft missile and gun shield over its ground forces, and treated all approaching aircraft as hostile. Despite its lack of sophistication, the system was apparently so 'effective' that a sizeable proportion of Iraqi aircraft downed during that conflict were the victims of 'friendly' fire! In this situation, compounded by the coalition's almost total destruction of Iraq's command and control system, it seems possible that any Iraqi aircraft that did take-off and head toward the front were engaged by both sides until they landed once more.

The task of the Iraqi air force's Air Support Command was support of surface operations by the army and navy. The Air Support Command therefore ran the operations of all attack, bomber and reconnaissance units within the air force. There is some dispute about the most effective aircraft in the Air Support Command inventory, the Sukhoi Su-24 'Fencer' interdictor, which is in the same class as the Tornado. If the Iraqi air force had tried to undertake an attack with chemical weapons against Israel or the coalition forces, the Su-24 would have been the type with the best chance of success. For this reason, therefore, the coalition air forces made a

Even Iraq's hardened aircraft shelters, built from reinforced concrete of considerable thickness, proved vulnerable to laser-guided weapons such as the 907 kg (2,000 lb) GBU-10I with its hardened steel casing

prime target of the air bases thought likely to support the Su-24, together with the hardened aircraft shelters accommodating these important aircraft. It was thought at the beginning of 1991 that the Iraqi air force had between 10 and 16 Su-24s (received shortly before the imposition of the UN's embargo on the delivery of weapons to Iraq) and it was only after the end of hostilities that Iraq revealed it had sent 24 Su-24s to Iran. This puts coalition intelligence in a poor light.

In a country with a generally poor transport infrastructure, air transport generally enjoys a high level of official support, and this was certainly the case with Iraq. The air

force had its own transport arm with some 45 aircraft, most of them supplied by the USSR. It could also call on the aircraft operated by the state-owned Iraqi Airways as well as some 40 freighters.

All battlefield helicopter units, and also all of Iraq's 'Scud' and other surface-to-surface missiles, were the responsibility of the army.

In trying to keep its mixed force of aircraft (acquired largely from France, the USSR and China – the last providing a number of Soviet types built in that country) at a high level of serviceability, the Iraqi air force faced major problems. Their greatest difficulty was that Iraq's aircraft were not bought to a planned system but rather on the basis of who was prepared to sell to Iraq when the necessary finance was available. As a result the Iraqi air force flew 15 different types of fixed-wing aircraft. Except for the Dassault Mirage F1, the Mikoyan-Gurevich MiG-21 'Fishbed' and the Sukhoi 'Fitter' (in its Su-7, Su-20 and Su-22 versions), orders had always totalled less than 60 aircraft. It was even worse in the case of the Iraqi forces' rotary-wing aircraft, for the air force and army between them flew no less than 16 types of helicopter.

There is no precise information on the serviceability rates of the aircraft in Iraqi service even before the occupation of Kuwait and the breakdown of relations with the rest of the world. However, the Iraqis are a technically capable and inventive people, and have shown themselves adept at keeping weapons serviceable under adverse conditions. It is possible, therefore, that the serviceability rates of the Iraqi air force were higher than was generally assumed, even though the implementation of the UN embargo must have made the task much harder, and forced the 'cannibalisation' of a few of each type of aircraft to keep the rest of the force airworthy.

According to a report from a Russian press agency on 25 January 1991 (unconfirmed by other sources) the commanding officers of the Iraqi air force and the Air Defence Command had both been shot for failing to perform their duties adequately. It is certain, however, that General Mezahim Sa'ib took over command of the Iraqi air force in this period.

During the course of the war that was shortly to erupt, some 148 Iraqi aircraft (including 115 warplanes) were flown to Iran.

The severe damage inflicted on Iraqi ammunition storage bunkers by McDonnell Douglas F-15Es is a testimony to this attack aircraft's excellent navigation, radar and FLIR systems, which can also be augmented by the two pods of the LANTIRN system for added night and adverse-weather capability at low level

The use of terrain-masked approaches was standard among the air units of the coalition forces to prevent the Iraqi air-defence system acquiring incoming aircraft through electronic, thermal or optronic means except at the last minute. The aircraft making this approach through typical desert terrain is a Vought A-7E Corsair II carrierborne attack aircraft of the VA-72 'Blue Hawks' squadron of CVW-3 deployed on the USS *John F. Kennedy (DoD via Robert F Dorr)*

It is believed that pilots of McDonnell Douglas F-15C Eagle fighters shot down at least five of the excellent Mikoyan-Gurevich MiG-29 'Fulcrum' fighters showing that in combat training and experience count as much as the theoretical capabilities of an aircraft and its weapons

History was now about to teach the Iraqi air force, in the most telling manner possible, that the mere possession of large numbers of aircraft does not give you an effective and combat-capable air arm. The Iraqi air force was perhaps combat-capable – but only by the standards of about 1970. Many of the Iraqi air force's aircraft dated from after that time, but the Iraqi air force had not learned, even in its long campaign against the Iranians, that weapons technology and air warfare thinking had progressed out of recognition since the 1970s. They were to enter combat against opponents who were not just more sophisticated in terms of their hardware but more importantly in terms of their air warfare thinking and training. There is no doubt that many of the Iraqi pilots flew and fought with courage and determination, but they were outclassed by the planners and pilots of the coalition air forces, which were the best units that the various members of the coalition could provide. In the circumstances, therefore, the coalition air units made their success over the Iraqi air force seem comparatively easy. As General Tony Peak, USAF chief-of-staff, later put it: 'I think [the Iraqi air force] did rather well under the circumstances. They're a pretty good outfit. They happened to be the second-best air force in the fracas. Having the second-best air force is like having the second-best poker hand - it's often the best strategy to fold early. I think they folded early.'

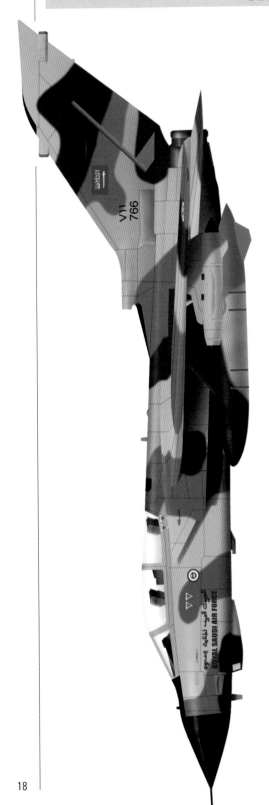

1
Panavia Tornado IDS interdictor, s/n 766, Royal Saudi Air Force

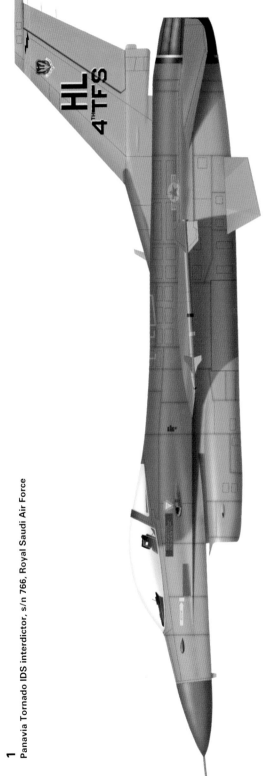

2
General Dynamics F-16C Fighting Falcon, 4th Tactical Fighter Squadron, US Air Force

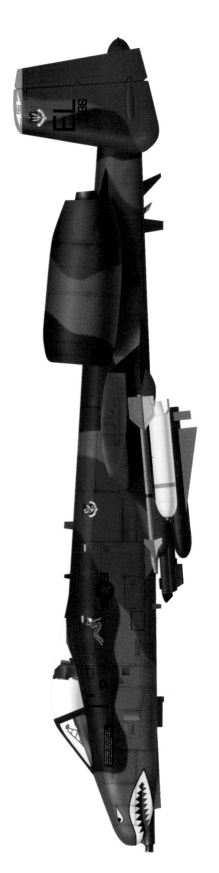

3

Fairchild Republic A-10A Thunderbolt II anti-tank and close support aircraft, s/n 80-186 'Tiger 1', 23rd Tactical Fighter Wing, US Air Force

4

McDonnell Douglas F-15C Eagle, s/n 82-046, 27th Tactical Fighter Sqn, US Air Force

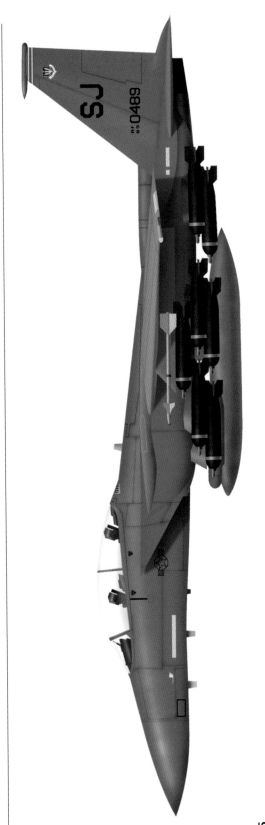

5
McDonnell Douglas F-15E Eagle, s/n 89-0489, 335 Tactical Fighter Squadron, US Air Force

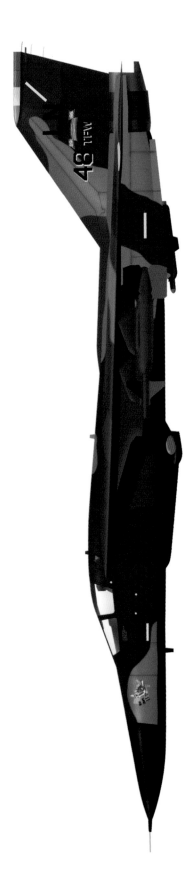

6
General Dynamics F-111F, s/n 70-2390 'Miss Liberty II', 494th Tactical Fighter Sqn, US Air Force

7
Lockheed F-117A Night Hawk, s/n 813 'Toxic Avenger', 415-416th Tactical Fighter Sqns, US Air Force

8
Boeing B-52G Stratofortress heavy bomber, s/n 58-0204, 379th Bomb Wing, US Air Force

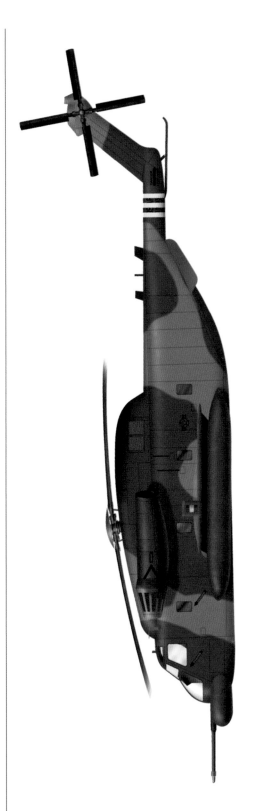

9
Sikorsky MH-53J 'Pave Low', s/n unknown, Special Operations Sqns, US Air Force

10
McDonnell Douglas F/A-18C Hornet, s/n 163508, VFA-81 'Sunliners' Sqn, US Navy

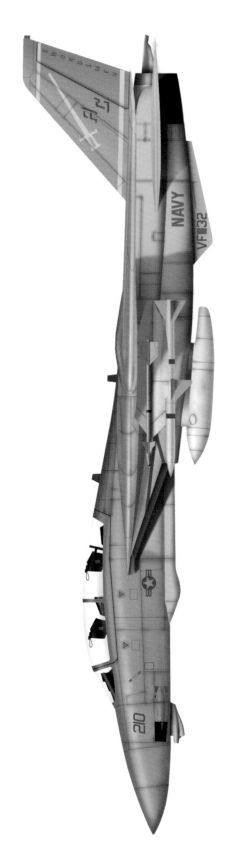

11
Grumman F-14A Tomcat, VF-32 'Swordsmen' Sqn, US Navy

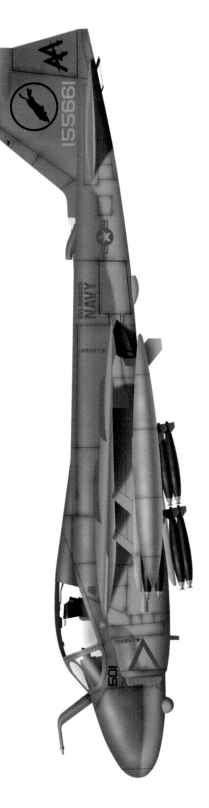

12
Grumman A-6E Intruder, s/n 155661, VA-35 'Black Panthers' Sqn, US Navy

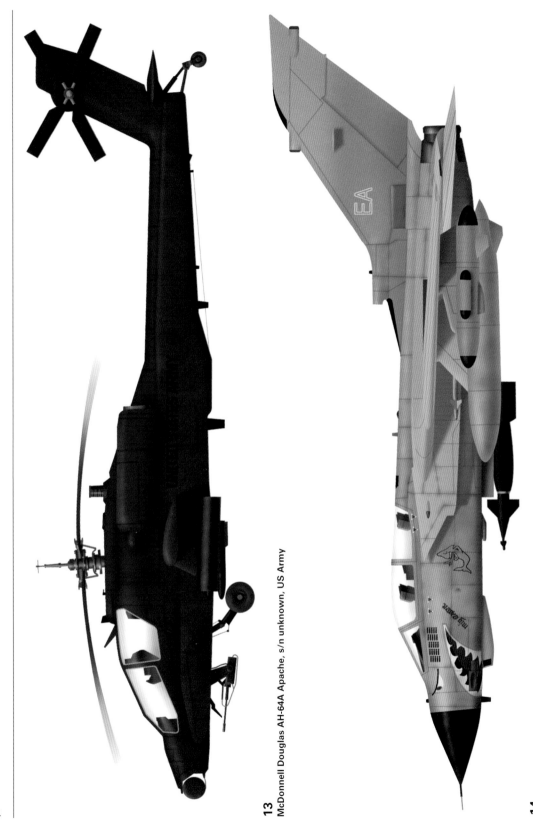

13
McDonnell Douglas AH-64A Apache, s/n unknown, US Army

14
Panavia Tornado GR 1 interdictor, s/n ZA477 'MiG Eater', RAF

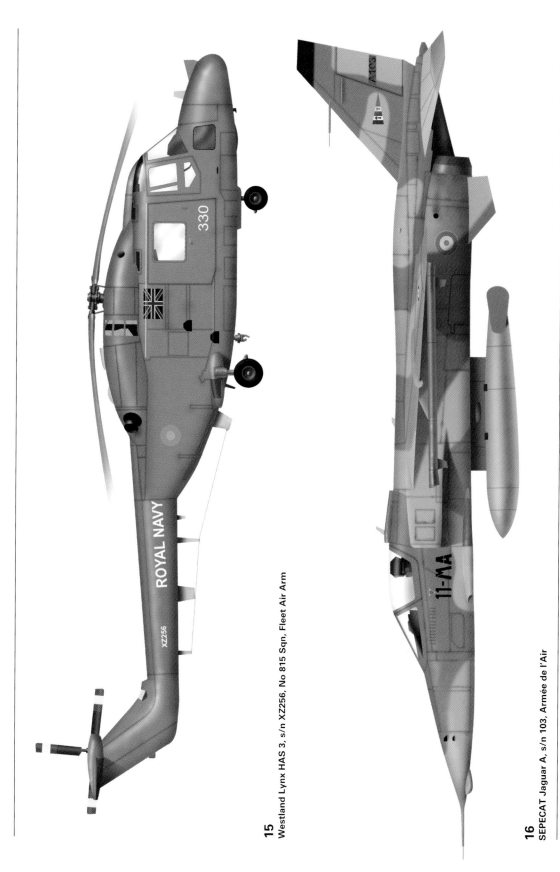

15
Westland Lynx HAS 3, s/n XZ256, No 815 Sqn, Fleet Air Arm

16
SEPECAT Jaguar A, s/n 103, Armée de l'Air

1

2

3

4

5

6

7

8

9

10

11

12

THE COALITION GATHERS: 1990

General H. Norman Schwarzkopf was the US Army officer selected to lead the coalition forces, with a British officer, Lieutenant General Sir Peter de la Billière, as his deputy. The largest number of aircraft available to the coalition forces' command for offensive operations into Iraq when hostilities finally broke out were from the US Air Force and the US Navy, supplemented by aircraft from the US Marine Corps and the US Army. There follows an assessment of some of the non-American units that made a contribution to the coalition.

SUPPORT FROM THE BRITISH

Other than the USA, the first nation to respond to the Saudi government's request for support in the face of possible Iraqi aggression was the UK. The British government was quick to condemn Iraq's initial aggression against Kuwait, and almost immediately followed this with the open decision to send air, land and sea units to bases in the states on the western side of the Persian Gulf. This plan got off the ground on 9 August 1990 when Tom King, the Secretary of State for Defence in the Conservative government, announced that the first tranche of the British effort would comprise 12 Tornado F 3 interceptors and 12 Jaguar GR 1A attack aircraft. The Tornados were already in Cyprus for an armament practice camp, and the Jaguars were in a state of constant readiness for short-notice deployment. This allowed the aircraft to depart to the Middle East with considerable speed.

The code name allocated to the RAF's reinforcement of the Middle East was Operation 'Granby', and implementation was entrusted to Air Chief Marshal Sir Patrick Hine, the Air Officer Commander-in-Chief of RAF Strike Command with its headquarters at High Wycombe some 30 miles (48 km) west of London. In Riyadh, Saudi Arabia, Air Vice Marshal 'Sandy' Wilson became the first Air Commander British Forces Arabian Peninsula before this role was taken over on 17 November by Air Vice Marshal W J 'Bill' Wratten. Initially commanding all the British forces in the theatre, the air commander became second-in-command to the army's

Carrying an underwing load of cluster bombs, a Vought A-7E Corsair II of the US Navy is caught on the moment of launch commitment from the flight deck of an aircraft carrier

Though optimised for the attack and reconnaissance role with a considerable weight of mission equipment on its one underfuselage and four underwing hardpoints, the SEPECAT Jaguar GR 1A clearly needed a self-protection capability against attacking aircraft, and therefore carried a pair of AIM-9 Sidewinder short-range AAMs on its two overwing hardpoints

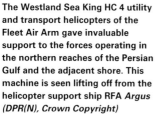

The Westland Sea King HC 4 utility and transport helicopters of the Fleet Air Arm gave invaluable support to the forces operating in the northern reaches of the Persian Gulf and the adjacent shore. This machine is seen lifting off from the helicopter support ship RFA *Argus* (DPR(N), Crown Copyright)

senior officer when Lieutenant General Sir Peter de la Billière became commander of British Forces Middle East on 1 November.

The build-up of the British air component at Dhahran Air Base (AB) in Saudi Arabia began on 9 August with the arrival of essential administrative and support personnel by Lockheed TriStar, and it was two days later that the first Tornado squadron arrived. As with all other RAF detachments to the Persian Gulf theatre, this squadron comprised aircraft and personnel from more than one unit, and was thus named No 5 (Composite) Squadron because the senior officer was the commanding officer of that unit.

The Tornado F 3 interceptors were at first used with aircraft of the USAF and the Royal Saudi Air force in carrying out four-hour combat air patrols (CAPs) along the Saudi border with Iraq and Kuwait. During the course of these CAPs, the Tornado interceptors were refuelled in the air by BAe VC10 tankers which arrived at Bahrain on 27 August. VC10s also delivered the personnel and initial equipment of the Jaguar squadron to Thumrait Air Base in Oman on 13 August, then moved to Seeb Air Base on 29 August. Given the distance of Oman from the probable location of physical actions against Iraq, the Jaguar unit was moved farther north, to Bahrain, between 7 and 10 October. Back at Seeb, three

33

BAe Nimrod MR 2 maritime patrol aircraft arrived from 13 August to co-operate with coalition warships in the maritime blockade of Iraq.

Up to this time the Jaguar constituted the only offensive element of the British contribution to the coalition air force, but on 23 August, the Ministry of Defence announced that a squadron of Tornado GR 1 interdictors would be despatched. Departing from bases in Germany on 27 August, the composite unit made for Bahrain, the aircraft already sporting the desert pink camouflage first seen on

the Jaguar. Tasked with attacking Iraqi air bases, the Tornado GR 1 suffered serviceability problems related to heat and sand, though these were eventually overcome. A second squadron, whose despatch was announced on 14 September, departed for Bahrain in two elements on 19 and 26 September, but later moved to Tabuk Air Base in the west of Saudi Arabia on 8 October.

The deployment of Tornado GR 1s was increased to three squadrons shortly before the 'Desert Shield' build-up turned into the 'Desert Storm' operation and the third unit reached Dhahran on 3 and 4 January 1991. Six Tornado GR 1As, with reconnaissance rather than interdiction as their primary responsibility, reached Dhahran from 14 to 16 January. The British forces for offensive air operations thus totalled some 50 Tornados and 12 Jaguars at three bases.

This was only part of the British build-up, however, for a Lockheed Hercules detachment came into existence at Riyadh on 1 November 1990 as the core of an in-theatre distribution network for the mass of supplies now being delivered in increasingly large quantities by Hercules, VC10 C 1 and TriStar transport aircraft. The strength of this Hercules unit was boosted to nine aircraft by the middle of January 1991, including two supplied and crewed by the Royal New Zealand Air Force. Another five Hercules transports operated from a base in the United Arab Emirates to support covert operations.

Carrying the Marconi Sky Shadow jammer and BOZ-107 chaff/flare dispenser pods under the outboard wing pylons, this Panavia Tornado GR 1 of No 14 Squadron is leaving its hardened aircraft shelter at RAF Brüggen, Germany, for the flight to Bahrain/Muharraq, where it became part of No 15 (Composite) Squadron (PRM)

The Tornado F 3 air-superiority fighter's counterparts were the Tornado GR 1 long-range interdictor and, as seen here, the Tornado GR 1A reconnaissance type. Provided by No 2 Squadron at Laarbruch in Germany, the latter has a horizon-to-horizon IR system in place of the interdictor's two 27 mm cannon, and in addition to two drop tanks carries under the outboard wing pylons a Marconi Sky Shadow ECM pod and a BOZ-107 chaff/flare dispenser pod respectively (DPR (RAF), Crown Copyright)

Logistic and personnel support for the British forces in the field were provided by the Lockheed Hercules in its C 1P short- and C 3P long-fuselage forms each fitted with an inflight refuelling probe over the flight deck

Inflight refuelling is an essential part of modern air warfare: this is the view from the navigator's (rear) seat of a Panavia Tornado as his pilot flies the aircraft's starboard-side probe into the basket drogue at the end of the fuel pipe lowered from a BAe Victor K 2 tanker

The RAF's in-theatre VC10 tankers (both K 2 and K 3 variants) were bolstered from 14 December by BAe Victor K 2 aircraft as they started to arrive at Bahrain. Six Victor tankers were available by 16 January, by which time the VC10 force of nine aircraft had been at Riyadh for a month.

Strengthening of the RAF in the theatre after the air war had started was designed to remedy the force's perceived lack of any precision attack capability with laser-guided bombs. The RAF Tornado attack aircraft could carry such weapons but lacked the means to designate the target, so 12 elderly BAe Buccaneer S 2Bs, each equipped with the 'Pave Spike' laser-designation pod, were flown to Bahrain, with the first two aircraft arriving on 26 January. These aircraft provided the required illumination capability for the laser-guided bombs of Tornados based at Bahrain and Dhahran, but those based at Tabuk co-operated with

Carrying the standard 'desert pink' camouflage of British aircraft allocated to the coalition air force, this SEPECAT Jaguar GR 1A based at Bahrain is already armed with two AIM-9 Sidewinder short-range AAMs and two CBU-87 cluster bombs above and below the wing respectively, and is about to be fitted with an ALQ-101(V) radar jamming pod under the outer hardpoint below the outboard wing pylon *(Mike Rondot via PRM)*

five specially equipped Tornado GR 1s that arrived from 6 February together with two TIALD (Thermal Imaging Airborne Laser Designation) acquisition/designation pods. In overall terms, therefore, the RAF in the Middle East had available to it a total of 62 Tornado GR 1/1As out of at least 87 that were earmarked for such service and accordingly painted in desert pink camouflage.

SUPPORT FROM THE FRENCH

France also decided at an early date that it would join the coalition. On 9 August the French government decided that sensible first moves would be the strengthening of its forces already in the Republic of Djibouti, as ordained by treaty with this former French colony on the western shores of the Gulf of Aden, and the forward movement of at least part of its Force d'Action Extérieure (FAE, or rapid deployment force), including the support and attack helicopters essential for modern mobile operations. Two days later additional elements were also sent to Djibouti to boost the capabilities of the Armée de l'Air units already there. These elements included secondary assets such as mobile radar, Crotale surface-to-air missile systems and Transall C.160NG transport aircraft modified for the inflight refuelling role, and primary assets such as the Dassault Mirage F1C fighters of Escadron de Chasse 4/30 'Vexin' and the Aérospatiale Alouette II helicopters and C.160 transport aircraft of Escadron de Transport d'Outre Mer 88 normally allocated to Détachement Air 188. These reinforcements were deemed sufficient to stabilise French interests in the Horn of Africa, but during this period the worsening situation in the Middle East soon persuaded the French government that it should start to make a contribution to the coalition forces now beginning to assemble in Saudi Arabia and neighbouring Persian Gulf states.

Seen here on the ground below a hovering Aérospatiale Puma HC 1 utility transport helicopter, the Aérospatiale Gazelle AH 1 flew unarmed to scout for the armed Lynx AH 7

How exactly to react was a more difficult question, for France's general policy was to a pursue a line independent of any major power bloc, and there were major figures in the French establishment (including Jean-Pierre Chevènement, the minister of defence) who wanted, for a variety of reasons, to find a compromise favourable to Iraq.

The French operation to build up its forces in Saudi Arabia was codenamed 'Salamandre', but the indeterminate nature of the French commitment to the theatre meant that it was nearly two months before the various components of the FAE and their helicopters became firmly based in and around the King Khalid Military City in north-eastern Saudi Arabia not far from the border with occupied Kuwait. The peripatetic nature of the French commitment is shown by the fact that the first elements started to move on 10 August 1990, only eight days after the Iraqi occupation of Kuwait. These elements comprised 30 Aérospatiale Gazelle light and 12 Aérospatiale Puma medium helicopters of the Aviation Légère de l'Armée de Terre's (ALAT) 5ème Régiment d'Hélicoptères de Combat (RHC), allocated to the FAE, and arrived on the French navy's aircraft carrier *Clemenceau* from Toulon. The embarkation of this force meant that the carrier had to leave in France much of its normal fixed-wing air strength (Vought Crusader fighter and Dassault Super Etendard attack aircraft), retaining only its four Dassault Alizé anti-submarine aircraft and a pair of Aérospatiale AS 365F Dauphin planeguard and SAR helicopters. The carrier sailed on 13 August, in case evacuation of French nationals from Kuwait should prove necessary. The carrier passed along the Suez Canal into the Red Sea but then remained at Djibouti from 22 to 28 August while the ALAT helicopters participated in training exercises with the forces already in Djibouti. As the carrier then sailed round the Arabian peninsula further exercises were undertaken with the forces of the United Arab Emirates as the ship called at Fujairah and Abu Dhabi, before it sailed back to the Red Sea and the port of Yanbu on Saudi Arabia's western coast.

At Yanbu the helicopters were landed for overland delivery to their Saudi Arabian bases. Logistic support was provided by three C.160F and C.160NG transport aircraft of Escadre de Transport 61 and ET 62, which reached Yanbu late in August and moved to the Riyadh International Airport early in October. On 9 September (two weeks before the *Clemenceau*'s docking at Yanbu) an Air France Boeing 747F freighter had joined two Hercules and four C.160F transports of the French air force in delivering two Aérospatiale SA 330B Puma medium and four SA 342M Gazelle light helicopters of the 3ème RHC, together with part of the regiment's personnel, direct to Yanbu from France.

After the Iraqi occupation forces in Kuwait forced their way into the French embassy, the French government decided to offer a more significant contribution to the coalition forces assembling in Saudi Arabia. The *Clemenceau* finally unloaded her helicopters between 22 and 25 September, and a few days later the heavy equipment for the 6ème Division Légère Blindée (light armoured division) arrived by ship from France to be manned by 4,200 personnel airlifted from the division's base near Nîmes to positions in the north-eastern part of Saudi Arabia.

All 48 French helicopters flew to the King Khalid Military City on 26 September, and two C.160 transport aircraft delivered HOT anti-tank missiles for the SA 342M machines from Djibouti to the same destination.

Armed with Magic short-range AAMs, this is a Dassault Mirage 2000C of the French air force's EC 5 unit. Until a late stage of the coalition's preparations for offensive operations against Iraq there was uncertainty as to whether or not the French units in Saudi Arabia would be committed by their government (via Ian Black)

Four days later, on 30 September, the ALAT declared operational its force of nine SA 341F/Canon gunship, nine SA 341F scout, 32 SA 342M Gazelle/HOT anti-tank and 18 SA 330B Puma helicopters.

This completed the first phase of French reinforcement for Saudi Arabia, but already plans had been laid for further French military strength to be delivered into the theatre. The second wave (loaded at Toulon onto four merchant ships) comprised 20 SA 342M helicopters of the 1ère and 5ème RHCs, based at Phalsbourg and Pau respectively, together with four SA 330B helicopters of the 4ème Régiment d'Hélicoptères de Commandement, de Manoeuvre et de Soutien (command, transport and support helicopter regiment) based at Nancy. The third wave of 40 more helicopters (including the Orchidée experimental machine with ground surveillance radar) followed at the beginning of the war.

Exasperated by the Iraqi entry into the French embassy in Kuwait, President François Mitterrand decided on 14 September that France should also make a contribution to the coalition's fixed-wing aircraft strength. On the next day the Armée de l'Air began Operation 'Daguet', the despatch of aircraft and personnel under the command of Général de Brigade Aérienne Jean-Pierre Gellibert. Unlike the American and British delivery of aircraft to Saudi Arabia, that of the French was notably slow, wholly as a result of continued political hedging. The first four Dassault

Longer-range missions by French aircraft were facilitated by the availability of Boeing C-135FR inflight refuelling tankers

Mirage 2000C fighters of the 5ème Escadre de Chasse at Base Aérienne 115 (Orange-Caritat) and four Dassault Mirage F1CR reconnaissance aircraft of the 33ème Escadre de Reconnaissance at BA 124 (Strasbourg-Entzheim) did not lift off from the staging point provided by BA 125 (Istres-Le Tubé) until 3 October, together with two Boeing C-135FR tankers of the 93ème Escadre de Ravitaillement en Vol. The eight aircraft refuelled three times in the course of their 2,750 miles (4,425 km) flight to Al Ahsa Airport, a civilian establishment outside Al Hufuf some 225 miles (360 km) south of Kuwait. There they came under the command of Colonel Jean-Pierre Job (promoted to général de brigade aérienne on 1 December) under the overall local command of the Commandement des Eléments Français (French command) located in Riyadh under Général de Corps d'Armée Roquejeoffre with Gellibert as his deputy for air matters.

Even as the units of the ALAT, Commandement Air des Forces de Défense Aérienne (CAFDA, or air defence command) and Force Aérienne Tactique (FATac, or tactical air command) were deploying into Saudi Arabia, the Commandement du Transport Aérienne Militaire (CoTAM, or military air transport command) inaugurated support flights between France and Saudi Arabia. The command's C.160, C-130H and DC-8-72 aircraft were aided by chartered civil aircraft. The CoTAM also created an in-theatre network of logistic flights, beginning with an initial deployment of three C.160 aircraft to Yanbu early in October 1990. This logistic network eventually increased to five C.160s that were later based at the incomplete Terminal 4 of Riyadh International Airport. This also became the base for the C-135FR inflight refu-elling tankers supplied by the Commandement de Forces Aérienne Stratégiques (CoFAS, or strategic air command) to support operations by tactical aircraft. After hostilities started, the C.160 force was increased to

One of the most tactically important contributions made by France to the coalition air campaign was its Dassault Mirage F1CR reconnaissance aeroplane. The type was also used, as illustrated here, as the bomb-carrying mothership for packages of less well equipped Jaguar A attack aircraft (background)

10 aircraft and bolstered by a pair of C-130H transports that were to keep mobile ground forces and their tactical air support supplied with equipment, food and ammunition.

Five days after the first French aircraft landed at Al Ahsa, a second group of four Mirage 2000C and four Mirage F1CRs arrived at the same base. On 15 and 17 October, these machines were complemented by two batches of four Jaguar A attack aircraft of EC 11 from the BA 136 (Toul-Rosières) base and, in November, by two SA 330Ba search-and-rescue helicopters of the Escadron d'Hélicoptères 1/67 'Pyrénées' from the BA 120 (Cazaux) base and one C.160G GABRIEL electronic reconnaissance aeroplane of the Escadron Electronique 54 'Dunkerque' from the BA 128 (Metz-Frescaty) base. French aircraft continued to arrive in the theatre, and by the time the UN deadline for the Iraqi departure from Kuwait arrived, the French air force had 24 Jaguars, 12 Mirage F1CRs, 12 Mirage 2000Cs, two Pumas and one C.160G at Al Ahsa in Saudi Arabia, together with light cannon mountings and SAM batteries for airfield defence. At Riyadh there were five C-135FR tankers, five C.160 transports, one Dassault Mystère 20 command transport and one Aérospatiale N262 liaison aeroplane. The French air force also positioned, at the King Khalid Military City, one Système de Détection de Contrôle Tactique (SDCT, or tactical detection and control system) radar protected by Crotale SAMs.

As soon as they had arrived at Al Ahsa, the pilots of tactical aircraft began in-theatre familiarisation flights leading the way to the operation of CAPs, of which the first was flown on 12 December with the support of C-135FR tankers for inflight refuelling. At this time, when the coalition command was not yet certain that the French air elements would be committed to offensive operations after the expiry of the 15 January deadline, the most important French contribution was the reconnaissance capability provided by the Mirage F1CRs, whose Thomson-CSF Raphael side-looking radar and Super Cyclope IR linescanner provided an electronic and thermal 'look' deep into Iraq and Kuwait as the machines flew on the Saudi Arabian side of the border. In this way the French aircraft provided a capability complementary to that of the American RF-4C with the LOROP (Long-Range Oblique Photography) system.

OTHER MEMBERS OF THE COALITION

The British and French contributions were second only to that of the USA. The other nations that played a part in the coalition, and in shielding it from interference, are now treated alphabetically.

Argentina did not commit herself to any major active role, but provided one Boeing 707 transport aeroplane that operated on delivery flights between El Palomar and Riyadh, and two C-130 Hercules transports for service within the theatre. The destroyer ARA *Almirante Brown* was deployed in the Red Sea as part of the coalition's efforts to halt blockade-running, and lost her Aérospatiale Alouette III helicopter in a ditching on 1 November. Another Alouette III was based on the destroyer ARA *Spiro*. The helicopters were provided by the 1a Escuadrilla Aéronaval de Helicopteros.

Australia provided no land-based aircraft, their major contribution being confined at any one time to a pair of warships. The first pair were

Tasked primarily with the protection of Canadian warships operating in the Persian Gulf, McDonnell Douglas CF-18 Hornet fighters provided by three Canadian Armed Forces' squadrons were based at Doha in Qatar *(Canadian Dept of National Defense)*

the frigates HMAS *Adelaide* and HMAS *Darwin,* which each operated one S-70B Seahawk in addition to an unarmed Aérospatiale AS.550B Ecureuil provided by No 723 Squadron. In December the original two ships were succeeded by the similar frigate HMAS *Sydney* and the destroyer HMAS *Brisbane*: the latter an older ship without helicopter capability. The C-130E Hercules transport aircraft of No 37 Squadron normally based at RAAF Richmond in New South Wales, made a more limited contribution.

From late August Belgium contributed two C-130H Hercules transport aircraft of No 20 Squadron based at Melsbroek, used mainly for the removal of refugees from Jordan to Egypt. In September Belgium offered another four Hercules, but a plan to send F-16A fighters to the region foundered in the face of political opposition and the air force's revelation that the aircraft lacked adequate electronic countermeasures for service in the Middle East.

Canada's initial contribution was five Sikorsky CH-124 Sea King helicopters of No 423 Squadron. These machines were based on the destroyers HMCS *Athabaskan* and HMCS *Terra Nova* (two helicopters each) and the supply ship *Protecteur.* However, after Iraqi troops had gutted the Canadian embassy in Kuwait City, Canada announced that she would despatch 18 McDonnell Douglas CF-18A Hornet dual-role aircraft of No 409 Squadron from CFB Söllingen in Germany. These

41

flew to Qatar on 7 October as the main element of the Canadian Air Task Group. Their task was to protect the two Canadian warships operating in the area by interception, if required, of Iraqi Mirage F1EQ anti-ship aircraft armed with the AM.39 Exocet missile. A rotation meant that No 409 Squadron was replaced by No 439 Squadron also from Söllingen, and later again by No 441 Squadron from CFB Cold Lake. Other Canadian air assets involved in the coalition effort came to include two Canadair EC-144A Challenger machines of No 414 Squadron and one Lockheed CP-140 Aurora of the Greenwood Wing. One of the EC-144A machines was later redeployed to Muharraq, where a CC-130 Hercules transport also operated in the support role.

Egypt offered Mirage 2000 and F-16 Fighting Falcon fighters during October, but these were not deployed into Saudi Arabia.

Germany contributed no first-line elements to the coalition forces assembling in the Arabian peninsula, but nonetheless undertook a small support role with C.160D transport aircraft. From 1 November a modest number of these machines operated from RAF Mildenhall in England to deliver equipment to other USAF bases in Europe, thereby freeing American aircraft for service in the Arabian peninsula.

Greece's involvement with the coalition was limited to the frigate *Elli,* later replaced by the *Limnos,* which operated in the anti-blockade runner role in the Red Sea with two Agusta (Bell) AB.212ASV/ASW helicopters.

In Operation 'Locusta', Italy moved eight Tornado IDS interdictors of the 154° and 156° Gruppi from Gioia del Colle to Al Dhafra (Maqatra). The aircraft left Italy on 25 September, and were refuelled in the air en route to Abu Dhabi by VC10 tankers of the RAF. The detachment was declared operational on 6 October. Eight replacement aircraft were ferried out, again with British help (in this instance by Victor tankers) during November. The Italian naval contribution was four warships including the frigates *Libeccio, Orsa* and *Zeffiro.* Stationed in the Arabian Gulf, these ships each had provision for one AB.212ASV/ASW or Agusta (Sikorsky) ASH-3H helicopter provided by the 6° Reparto Elicotteri.

Kuwait, despite being occupied by Iraqi forces, was also able to make a contribution. A number of Kuwaiti pilots had escaped the advancing

The pilots of the 'Free Kuwait' A-4KU force flew with great determination against the Iraqi forces, and for a time before the outbreak of hostilities were denied weapons lest their aggressive patrolling spark open war before the coalition was ready *(Ian Black)*

As in every campaign involving the US Army and its allies since the early 1970s, the Boeing CH-47 Chinook played an invaluable role as a heavy personnel and logistic transport delivering items such as this piece of field artillery and its tractor

Iraqi forces in their aircraft, allowing the creation in Saudi Arabia of the 'Free Kuwait Air Force', which flew as an element of the Royal Saudi Air Force but retained Kuwaiti markings. The Free Kuwait Air Force comprised two composite squadrons at Dhahran, one with 18 A-4KU Skyhawk II single-seat and two TA-4KU Skyhawk II two-seat aircraft previously of Nos 9 and 25 Squadrons, and the other with 15 Mirage F1CK single-seat aircraft previously of Nos 18 and 61 Squadrons. Other available Kuwaiti aircraft included six BAe Hawk two-seat trainers and, based at Al Jubail, 22 Aérospatiale helicopters in the form of 12 SA 342K Gazelle, six SA 330 Puma and four AS 532C Cougar machines.

In September 1990 the Netherlands considered but did not implement the despatch of 18 F-16A Fighting Falcons flown by pilots of Nos 315 and 313 Squadrons based at Twenthe. The Dutch naval effort comprised a single frigate (HrMS *Pieter Florisz* replaced in November by HrMS *Philips van Almonde*) carrying two Westland Lynx helicopters.

New Zealand's contribution was C-130H aircraft and crews of No 40 Squadron at RNZAF Whenuapai; these were attached to the RAF air Transport Detachment at Riyadh/King Khalid International Airport.

A final European contribution to the Middle East was provided by the ACE Mobile Force, a component assigned to the Allied Command Europe. The Mobile Force is a multi-national NATO organisation created for 'fire brigade' rapid intervention duties for the protection of a member of the NATO alliance threatened with attack. Fearing the possibility of an Iraqi attack, Turkey requested support from the ACE Mobile force in December 1990. The air strength then deployed to Turkey as a result of an agreement on 2 January 1991 included 42 aircraft from Belgium, Germany and Italy: Germany contributed 18 Dornier/Dassault Alpha Jet A light attack aircraft of JBG 43 at Oldenburg, Belgium provided 18 Dassault Mirage 5BA attack aircraft of No 8 Squadron at Bierset, and Italy supplied six Lockheed RF-104G Starfighter reconnaissance aircraft of the 3° Stormo at Villafranca.

The Gulf states of Bahrain, Qatar, Saudi Arabia and the United Arab Emirates also contributed to the coalition air effort. Lastly, South Korea provided a C-130H transport from a squadron thought to have been based at Pusan.

BUILDING UP THE 'DESERT SHIELD'

As the United Nations' deadline of 15 January 1991 for Iraq to pull her forces out of Kuwait passed, 'Desert Shield' and the various other coalition operations had brought huge forces, air, land and sea, to Saudi Arabia and the Arab nations to her east and south-east. Large numbers of coalition aircraft were now in the theatre, and this strength was very much greater than the Arab states had anticipated for their own purposes. This meant that it was necessary, for example, to complete rapidly the conversion into military bases of some civil airports that were still under construction.

US AIR FORCE

The first US Air Force response to the Iraqi invasion of Kuwait had been the hasty despatch of several Tactical Air Command (TAC) defensive units from the USA to bolster the protection of strategic bases in the Gulf

Delivery and protection of the US Marine Corps' ground and air forces was the task of US Navy vessels such as the amphibious assault ship USS *Saipan*. The ship had a flight deck capable of accepting machines such as the Boeing CH-46 Sea Knight medium assault and utility helicopter (in the air), the Sikorsky CH-53 Sea Stallion heavy assault and logistic transport helicopter (left on the flight deck) and the McDonnell Douglas/BAe AV-8B Harrier II close air support aircraft (right on the flight deck)

The standard short-range weapon carried by the McDonnell Douglas F-15 Eagle and other American fighters was the AIM-9M Sidewinder missile, an effective missile with all-aspect engagement capability

region. This was followed by TAC offensive units to increase overall capability, allowing coalition planners to consider military moves to expel the Iraqi forces from Kuwait if diplomatic measures failed, and to deter the possibility of further Iraqi aggression.

After this further USAF units were moved to the theatre, mainly from the USA and Europe but with a smaller number from the Far East. One of the first units to arrive in Saudi Arabia was the 1st TFW, two of whose McDonnell Douglas F-15C Eagle air-superiority fighters flew into Dhahran AB, where they were later joined by the 58th TFS of the 33rd TFW from Eglin AFB, Florida, and by at least one squadron from Bitburg in Germany.

General Dynamics F-16C Fighting Falcon air combat and multi-role fighters from two squadrons of the 363rd TFW, home-based at Shaw AFB, South Carolina, deployed to Sharjah, and the 4th and 421st TFSs of the 388th TFW at Hill AFB, Utah, flew into a Saudi Arabian base to join the 69th TFS of the 347th TFW from Moody AFB, Georgia. Two F-16 units of the Air National Guard (ANG), in the form of the 138th TFS from Syracuse, New York, and the 157th TFS from McEntire, South Carolina, were called into active service and also self-deployed to the Persian Gulf theatre during December.

The 336th TFS of the 4th TFW flew from Seymour Johnson AFB, North Carolina, to Thumrait with its F-15E Eagle attack aircraft early in August, but then shifted to a new base in the eastern part of Saudi Arabia, where it was joined by its sister squadron, the 335th TFS. The Fairchild Republic A-10A Thunderbolt II gave further tactical close support and capable but daylight-only anti-tank capability. Aircraft of this type, operated by two squadrons of the 23rd TFW at England AFB, Louisiana, flew out on 27 August, and were followed in November by the OA-10A forward air control aircraft of the 602nd Tactical Air Control Wing (TACW) home-based at Davis-Monthan AFB, Arizona. On 27 December 18 more A-10As (from the 511th TFS of the 10th TFW at RAF Alconbury) flew out to the Gulf from England. At about the same time additional A-10A capability arrived in the theatre in the form of the 706th TFS of the 926th Tactical Fighter Group (TFG) of the Air Force Reserve (AFRes) normally based at Naval Air Station (NAS) New Orleans, Louisiana.

The 561st TFS of the 35th TFW (George AFB, California) flew to Saudi Arabia in its specially equipped McDonnell Douglas F-4G Phantom II 'Wild Weasel' aircraft, arriving on 16 August for the SEAD (Suppression of Enemy Air Defences) role vital to the reduction of the enemy's surface-based threat to other attacking aircraft. It was soon supplemented in this vital role by the identical aircraft of the 52nd TFW's 23rd TFS usually based at Spangdahlem AB, Germany.

Control of these and other air assets was entrusted to a force of five Boeing E-3B/C Sentry AWACS aircraft provided by the 552nd Airborne Warning & Control System (AW&CS) Wing, from Tinker AFB, Oklahoma. These were airborne on an almost continual basis and, in order to avoid severe inroads into the fatigue lives of these essential 'force multiplier' aircraft, the Sentries were rotated back to the USA on a weekly basis.

Another high-technology air asset rapidly deployed to Saudi Arabia was the Lockheed F-117A Night Hawk 'stealth' attack aircraft of the 415th TFS of the 37th TFW from its classified base on the Tonopah Test Range in the vast Nellis AFB in Nevada. The first 20 of these aircraft, which were virtually impossible for the Iraqis to track and therefore to engage in the air, arrived at Khamis Mushait AB deep in south-western Saudi Arabia, on 20 August. The US Secretary of Defense, Dick Cheney revealed in November that another F-117A squadron would soon be operating in the Gulf theatre, in the form of the 416th TFS.

A tactical and operational capability which the USAF could not adequately provide was reconnaissance. To bolster the coalition's ability to detect and locate accurately the huge strength of men, armour and artillery that the Iraqis were massing on their side of the border with Saudi Arabia and in Kuwait, the USA activated a number of ANG units. The first of these was the 117th Tactical Reconnaissance Wing's 106th Tactical Reconnaissance Squadron (TRS) of the Alabama ANG, whose RF-4C Phantom IIs flew into the Persian Gulf theatre from its home at Birmingham Municipal Airport only a few days after the start of the crisis. The 152nd Tactical Reconnaissance Group's 192nd TRS from Reno, Nevada, reached Saudi Arabia on 1 December.

All the other ANG units activated at an early stage of the 'Desert Shield' build-up were transport and inflight-refuelling tanker outfits flying Lockheed C-130 Hercules and Boeing KC-135 Stratotanker aircraft respectively. In December, however, two F-16A fighter units of the ANG were called into action, these being the 169th TFG's 157th TFS at McEntire ANGB, South Carolina, and 174th TFW's 138th TFS at Syracuse/Hancock International Airport, New York. At this same stage of 'Desert Shield', with plans now firmly based on the need for offensive rather than defensive action, the 926th TFG's 706th TFS was activated at NAS New Orleans. Equipped with A-10A aircraft, the 706th TFS was the first Air Force Reserve fighter unit ever activated.

To supplement the efforts of the F-4G SEAD aircraft, the USAF also moved to Saudi Arabia the Grumman (General Dynamics) EF-111A Raven electronic warfare aircraft of the 41st Electronic Combat Squadron (ECS) of the 66th Electronic Combat Wing (ECW) from RAF

A major contribution to the coalition air effort against Iraq was made by the Lockheed F-117A 'stealth' attack aircraft of the 37th Tactical Fighter Wing based well beyond Iraqi retaliatory efforts at Khamis Mushait Air Base in the south-western corner of Saudi Arabia. The 37th TFW was tasked with the destruction of strategically vital targets such as Iraq's nuclear and biological weapons production centres as well as the devastation of Iraq's centralised command, control and communications capability *(DoD via Robert F Dorr)*

With a single Grumman A-6E Intruder in the background, eight Vought A-7E Corsair II attack aircraft wait to take on fuel from a Boeing KC-135 once the ninth aeroplane has topped off its tanks

Upper Heyford, England, and of the 366th ECW's 390th ECS from Mountain Home AFB, Idaho. The former unit was supplemented by the same wing's 43rd ECS with EC-130H aircraft normally based at Sembach AB in Germany.

Twelve ANG and AFRes transport squadrons were activated soon after the beginning of 'Desert Shield' to supplement the efforts of the USAF's Military Airlift Command (MAC). Included among these units were the 756th Military Airlift Squadron (MAS) of the 459th Military Airlift Wing (MAW) at Andrews AFB, Maryland, with the Lockheed C-141B StarLifter, along with 433rd MAW's 68th MAS at Kelly AFB, Texas, and the 439th MAW's 337th MAS at Westover AFB, Massachusetts, both operating the huge Lockheed C-5A Galaxy. The aircraft of these three AFRes squadrons were supplemented by those of two ANG squadrons, namely C-5A machines of the 105th Military Airlift Group's 137th MAS at Stewart ANGB, New York, and the C-141B machines of the 183rd MAG's 172nd MAS from Jackson Airport, Mississippi. Aircrew from at least five AFRes (Associate) squadrons were also made available to boost the numbers of personnel available for the heavy schedule of transport flights between the USA and the Persian Gulf theatre.

Five AFRes and three ANG transport squadrons flying the C-130 Hercules turboprop-powered tactical transport were activated either for service in the Gulf region or in Europe, where the availability of these reserve units allowed MAC C-130 transport assets to be redeployed to the Gulf. The C-130E and C-130H transport aircraft of MAC, the AFRes and ANG undertook the lion's share of transport within the Gulf region, but the main burden of flying equipment and personnel into the theatre from Europe and the USA was borne by the C-5 Galaxy and C-141 StarLifter fleets of turbofan-powered heavy transport aircraft. The airlift was a high-intensity effort to the primary bases in Saudi Arabia, namely Dhahran and Riyadh, but for lack of ramp area at these Saudi bases many of MAC's operations staged through Frankfurt/Rhein Main and Ramstein ABs in Germany as well as Torrejon AB in Spain. So intensive was the required effort that an estimated 3,400 sorties in the course of the first two months of the 'Desert Shield' were not adequate and additional capacity had to be provided by the Strategic Air Command (SAC), whose KC-135 tankers were operated in their seldom-employed secondary role as transports for the delivery of lighter weapons, equipment and personnel.

The daily rate of MAC sorties declined to about 70 from mid-September, allowing crews to be rested and their aircraft to receive deferred unit-level maintenance. It is worth noting that some 500 sorties to move heavy freight loads were undertaken by aircraft of the Civil Reserve Air Fleet during the first two months of 'Desert Shield'. The MAC also supplied two other units, the 375th MAW's 1401st and 1402nd MASs, with Learjet C-21A light transports in five detachments at the bases at Riyadh and the King Khalid Military City for the staff transport and liaison roles.

Ground crew prepare to change the Allison T56 turboprop engine in the starboard inner position of a Lockheed C-130 Hercules, the workhorse for the tactical airlift role in Operations 'Desert Shield' and 'Desert Storm'

Only a few weeks after it had become a command of its own, the Special Operations Command (SOC) despatched a number of different aircraft types to Saudi Arabia. These were initially the MC-130E machines of the 1st Special Operations Wing's 8th Special Operations Squadron (SOS) and the HC-130N/P machines of the same wing's 9th SOS, followed in September by the AC-130H 'Spectre' gunships of the wing's 16th SOS and then in November by the Sikorsky MH-53J and Sikorsky MH-60G helicopters of the wing's 20th and 55th SOSs. The 8th, 16th and 20th SOSs were moved up from Hurlburt Field in Florida, and the 9th and 55th SOSs from Eglin AFB, also in Florida.

As the American build-up continued more assets came from US Air Force Europe (USAFE). Three of the four squadrons of F-15C air-superiority fighters on the strength of USAFE were detached to the Middle East at the end of 1990 and the beginning of 1991. The squadrons were the 53rd and 525th TFS of the 36th TFW based at Bitburg AB in Germany, and the 32nd TFS of the 32nd TFG based at Soesterberg AB in the Netherlands. To bolster its strength the Royal Saudi Air Force received 24 F-15Cs from USAFE stocks.

Another tactical fighter deployed from Europe to the Middle East was the F-16C. The first such aircraft to reach the theatre, during the course of August, were the Fighting Falcons of the 401st TFW's 614th TFS normally based at Torrejon AB in Spain, and two later arrivals were the 50th TFW's 10th TFS, normally located at Hahn AB in Germany, and then the 401st TFW's 612th TFS. The first of the squadrons was then based at Doha, while the two later arrivals took up station at Incirlik AB in Turkey.

The primary heavy search-and-rescue helicopter operated by the US Air Force from Saudi bases was the Sikorsky MH-53J. It was well armoured and armed, featured a retractable inflight refuelling probe as well as drop tanks for additional range, and possessed a cockpit fitted with advanced sensors and instruments for low-level flight in all weather conditions

The General Dynamics F-111F 'Aardvark', flown from Taif by the three squadrons of the 48th Tactical Fighter Wing from RAF Lakenheath in England, was one of the most important heavy attack aircraft deployed by the coalition. This machine was fitted with an example of the GBU-28/B 'Deep Throat'. Weighing some 2,132 kg (4,700 lb), this was the heaviest weapon carried by the F-111. It was a deep-penetration weapon created from surplus 203 mm (8 in) gun barrels bored out, filled with explosive, and fitted with a laser-guidance package for attacks against hardened targets such as command centres

The most successful bomber of the forthcoming air campaign over Kuwait and Iraq was undoubtedly the F-111, which was able to deliver substantial warloads of 'dumb' (unguided) and 'smart' (guided) weapons, the latter in the form of the 'Paveway' series of laser-guided bombs using the bomber's own laser designation system in addition to third-party illumination of the target. The first such aircraft to reach the theatre in August 1990 were the F-111Fs of the 48th TFW normally based at RAF Lakenheath in England. This wing deployed the machines of its 492nd, 493rd and 494th TFSs to Taif in Saudi Arabia during August 1990, and the first F-111E machines of the 20th TFW, normally based at RAF Upper Heyford in England, arrived the same month at Incirlik AB. Although this wing's 79th TFS was the lead unit, elements of its other two squadrons, the 55th and 77th TFSs, were rotated through Incirlik. Another but somewhat differently tasked variant of the F-111 released from USAFE strength to bolster the coalition effort in the Middle East was the EF-111A electronic combat model, which the 42nd ECS operated from Incirlik after detachment from the 66th ECW's base at RAF Upper Heyford.

Another asset deemed essential to the success of the imminent coalition air effort was the heavy bombing capability of the Boeing B-52G Stratofortresses of the Strategic Air Command (SAC) in the USA. The first move to provide a heavy bomber force for service over the Middle East was the creation of a provisional bomb wing (BW[P]) at Diego Garcia, the British-owned island in the Indian Ocean on which the Americans had built a major forward base, to supervise the efforts of two detached squadrons. Arriving in August, these were the 69th Bomb Squadron (BS) of the 42nd Bomb Wing (BW) normally based at Loring AFB in Maine and the 328th Bomb Training Squadron of the 93rd BW normally based at Castle AFB in California. These two squadrons moved to Jeddah/King Abdul Aziz International Airport in January, their place on Diego Garcia being taken by the 97th BW's 340th BS normally located at Eaker AFB in Arizona. King Abdul Aziz International Airport was also home, at times, to the 2nd BW's 62nd and 596th BSs from Barksdale AFB in Louisiana, the 379th BW's 524th BS from Wurtsmith

AFB in Michigan and the 416th BW's 668th BS from Griffiss AFB in New York, although with their very long range and inflight refuelling capability, the aircraft of these three squadrons also operated from RAF Fairford in England and Moron AB in Spain.

The other primary SAC assets deployed for service in the Middle East were reconnaissance and intelligence-gathering aircraft, and inflight refuelling tankers. The reconnaissance force was based on the Lockheed U-2R and TR-1A, two types operated by the 99th Strategic Reconnaissance Squadron (SRS) of the 9th Strategic Reconnaissance Wing (SRW). Normally located at Beale AFB in California, the 99th SRS from August flew from Taif in Saudi Arabia with a detachment at RAF Akrotiri on the island of Cyprus. Taif was also the temporary home for the TR-1A aircraft of the 17th Reconnaissance Wing's 95th Reconnaissance Squadron, normally to be found at RAF Alconbury in England. Intelligence gathering was the responsibility of the Boeing RC-135U/V/W aircraft operated from Riyadh and the King Khalid Military City by the 343rd SRS of the 55th SRW, a unit normally based at Offutt AFB in Nevada. Another reconnaissance asset making its first operational appearance at this time, even though the type was still under development, was the Boeing E-8A Joint-STARS operational- and tactical-level reconnaissance platform. For service in the Middle East the 4411th J-STARS Squadron was detached from Melbourne in Florida by the Air Force Systems Command for service from Riyadh and the King Khalid Military City.

The other main responsibility of the SAC was inflight refuelling, primarily for the command's own aircraft but to a lesser but growing extent the tactical aircraft operated by other commands. The machines were McDonnell Douglas KC-10A Extender dual-role tanker and transport aircraft flown by five squadrons, and KC-135 tanker aircraft flown by no fewer than 30 squadrons. The operations of all tanker aircraft, including those of the AFRes and ANG, were controlled locally by several specially created Air Refueling Wings (Provisional) set up at bases in Egypt, Saudi Arabia and Oman.

US NAVY

Even as the USAF was implementing its first hastily created plan to provide air reinforcement to Saudi Arabia, the US Navy was also responding to presidential command, via the Department of Defense, in pushing several

With its exceptional range, even when carrying massive loads of free-fall 'iron' bombs, the Boeing B-52 Stratofortress could operate effectively from bases well outside the theatre, simplifying the logistic complexity of basing large numbers of different aircraft types in Saudi Arabia and neighbouring countries. This B-52G was photographed at RAF Fairford in England, which provided a temporary home for eight Stratofortress bombers

aircraft carrier battle groups into the waters of the Persian Gulf and Red Sea to provide additional strength in any air/land campaign and also to strengthen the embargo on goods and weapons being delivered by sea directly to Iraq or indirectly through the Jordanian port of Aqaba for overland final movement to Iraq. The US Navy Middle East Group, headed by the command ship USS *La Salle* along with its supporting cruiser, destroyer and frigate force, was undertaking an exercise in the Persian Gulf even as Iraq seized Kuwait, and was therefore the first US force in position to respond to further Iraqi aggression.

Reacting with commendable speed, the US Navy rapidly assembled four carrier battle groups in the theatre. USS *Independence* had been in the Gulf of Oman already while the nuclear-powered USS *Dwight D. Eisenhower* was in the Mediterranean on a cruise which was curtailed so that the ship could sail for the Red Sea on 8 August. The third carrier battle group was based on the USS *Saratoga,* which departed from Norfolk, Virginia, on 7 August and steamed at high speed across the Atlantic and into the Mediterranean. From there she, like the *Dwight D. Eisenhower,* passed south through the Suez Canal on 23 August. Included in the *Saratoga*'s battle group was the battleship USS *Wisconsin.* The *Eisenhower* had sailed from the USA on 8 March and was scheduled to return to the USA later in the summer. To enable the

Although the Boeing KC-135 Stratotanker was designed for the refuelling of US Air Force aircraft with a rigid flying boom that was extended into the upper-fuselage receptacle of the aircraft, the need to refuel tactical aircraft of the US Navy and US Marine Corps, such as this Grumman A-6E Intruder, led to the development of a short hose-and-drogue attachment

Dwight D. Eisenhower's cruise to be completed within a reasonable time, the US Navy despatched the USS *John F. Kennedy* to the Gulf at very short notice. The ship sailed on 15 August and arrived in the region early in September. Once the *John F. Kennedy* was on station, the *Dwight D. Eisenhower* sailed for the USA. The fourth aircraft carrier involved in 'Desert Shield' was the elderly USS *Midway,* which left its home port of Yokosuka, Japan, during September. The number of carriers in the theatre grew to six after the USS *America* and the nuclear-powered USS *Theodore Roosevelt* departed from the eastern coast of the USA late in December 1990.

Brought to a rapid halt after catching the arrester wire, this Grumman F-14A (Plus) Tomcat is identified by its markings as a machine of the VF-74 of the USS *Saratoga's* CVW-17 wing

An essential element in the effective tactical deployment of the US Navy's fighters was the Grumman E-2C Hawkeye airborne warning and control system aeroplane. The carrierborne counterpart of the USAF's Boeing E-3 Sentry, the E-2C had powerful radar with its antenna in a large rotodome above the fuselage, and could control many operations at long range

Each of these aircraft carriers had on board a carrier air wing. All except those on the *Midway* and the *John F. Kennedy* used the Grumman F-14 Tomcat or McDonnell Douglas F/A-18 Hornet for air-superiority and offensive roles. Each carrier air wing also included single squadrons each operating the Grumman A-6E Intruder attack aircraft and its KA-6D Intruder inflight refuelling tanker counterpart, the Grumman E-2C Hawkeye airborne early warning and control aeroplane, the Grumman EA-6B Prowler electronic warfare counterpart of the A-6 Intruder, the Lockheed S-3 Viking anti-submarine aircraft, and the Sikorsky SH-3H

Grumman EA-6B Prowler electronic warfare aircraft of the US Navy's VAQ-132 squadron, a unit of the CVW-17 based on the carrier USS *Saratoga,* was one of the several disparate elements that went into the creation of attack packages able to find their way to and from targets without undue Iraqi interference

With no submarine threat to guard against, the Lockheed S-3 Viking could be adapted for other tasks. Here an S-3B of the USS *John F. Kennedy's* VS-22 squadron is operating in the 'buddy' tanker role with a hose-and-drogue unit to refuel a Vought A-7E Corsair II

For Operation 'Desert Storm', the USS *John F. Kennedy's* air wing included two squadrons equipped with the Vought A-7E Corsair II, a type making its swan song before retirement. This Corsair II carries retarded bombs under its wing and AIM-9 Sidewinder short-range AAMs on the two hardpoints on the sides of the fuselage under the wing leading edges

Sea King missile defence, planeguard and utility helicopter. Two of the carrier air wings flew the F-14A (Plus) variant of the Tomcat, while three operated the latest F/A-18C version of the Hornet. Of the Viking squadrons, four operated the latest S-3B variant rather than the original S-3A model. The carrier air wing of the USS *John F. Kennedy* included two attack squadrons flying the Vought A-7E Corsair II on the type's last deployment. The carrier air wing of the *Midway* was different again with three F/A-18A, two A-6E, one E-2C, one EA-6B and one SH-3H squadrons. The carrier air wing embarked on the *Theodore Roosevelt* conformed to the standard pattern with the exception of its attack component, which was boosted by the inclusion of a second A-6E Intruder squadron.

The *Independence* entered the Persian Gulf on 1 October for a training exercise, and this constituted the first entry into these waters by an American aircraft carrier since the USS *Constellation* in 1974.

With each carrier air wing possessing around 75 to 80 aircraft, the US Navy had between 450 and 500 carrierborne aeroplanes and helicopters available to it in the theatre. These were not the service's only assets in the theatre, however, for there were also a considerable number of helicopters embarked on the cruisers, destroyers and frigates around the Arabian peninsula, and on the various support and resupply vessels. Many of the larger warships carried either the Kaman SH-2F Seasprite or Sikorsky SH-60B Seahawk LAMPS (Light Airborne Multi-Purpose) Mk III helicopters for both defence and ship-to-shore duties. The support vessels, fitted with larger helicopter platforms, carried utility helicopters such as the Boeing UH-46 Sea Knight, while the USS *La Salle* normally embarked an SH-3G Sea King from the HC-2 squadron to provide staff transport and communications capabilities for the Commander Middle East Forces at his headquarters in Bahrain.

Several shore-based types were also available. The most important of these was the Lockheed P-3C Orion maritime patrol aeroplane, which flew sorties over the waters of the Persian Gulf, the Red Sea, the Gulf of Oman and the Arabian Sea from bases such as Jeddah, Bahrain and Masirah as well as Diego Garcia. It is believed that at least 13 Orion maritime patrol squadrons were involved in these operations, including units from as far afield as Naval Air Station (NAS) Barbers Point in Hawaii, the home of the VP-1 squadron. The Orion was also the basis of the US Navy's electronic intelligence-gathering operation in the theatre. The specific variant involved in this important task was the EP-3E flown from Bahrain by detachments of the VQ-1 and VQ-2 squadrons normally based at NAS Agana on the island of Guam in the Marianas group and at NAS Rota in southern Spain. VQ-2 also operated detachments from Jeddah and Soudha Bay in Crete with the older McDonnell Douglas EA-3B Skywarrior.

Chaff and flares, seen here in the form of reload packages for Grumman A-6E Intruder attack aircraft of the US Navy, were used in prodigious quantities in a generally successful effort to decoy Iraqi radar- and IR-seeking missiles away from coalition aircraft

The aircraft carrier USS *John F. Kennedy* operated as part of the US Navy's Red Sea Battle Group. The ship's embarked air wing was CVW-3, whose aircraft carried the letters 'AC' on their fins. The wing's nine squadrons were VF-33 and VF-102 with the Grumman F-14A Tomcat fighter, VA-46 and VA-72 with the Vought A-7E Corsair II, VA-75 with the Grumman A-6E and KA-6D Intruder, VAW-126 with the Grumman E-2C Hawkeye, VAQ-130 with the Grumman EA-6B Prowler, VS-22 with the Lockheed S-3A Viking, and HS-7 with the Sikorsky SH-3H Sea King

The US Navy relied on the MAC for the air delivery of larger and heavier freight loads, but relied on its own assets for the rapid movement of lighter loads such as passengers, urgent freight and mail for onward delivery to more than 100 ships operating in the theatre. This transport effort involved regular and reserve units. The VR-22 squadron at Rota flew the C-130F, and the several reserve units that flew the McDonnell Douglas C-9B from Naples in Italy and from Bitburg and Sembach in Germany included the VR-55 squadron from NAS Alameda, California, the VR-57 squadron from NAS North Island, California, the VR-58 squadron from NAS Jacksonville, Florida, and the VR-59 squadron from NAS Dallas, Texas. Carrier onboard delivery (COD) duties, linking shore bases with aircraft carriers, were the responsibility of the Grumman C-2A Greyhound, the aircraft being provided by the VR-24 squadron from NAS Sigonella, Sicily, the VCR-30 squadron from NAS North Island, the VRC-40 squadron from NAS Norfolk, Virginia, and the VRC-50 squadron from NAS Cubi Point, Philippines – the later also flew the US-3A. The US Navy's counterpart to the USAF's C-21 for the rapid movement of VIPs and staff officers was the Beech UC-12B, operated by the NARU Willow Grove from NAS Willow Grove, Pennsylvania.

US MARINE CORPS (USMC)

A capability for fast deployment has always been a hallmark of the USMC, and this capability was used to the full as the USA moved to reinforce Saudi Arabia as rapidly as possible in the early days of the crisis. Only six days after President Bush's order of 6 August, the USMC began to arrive in Saudi Arabia, and within four weeks the corps had 45,000 personnel in and around the port of Al Jubail. This initial 'Desert Shield' deployment was undertaken in accordance with the corps' Marine Air Ground Task Force concept, and the surface forces were complemented by more than 200 fixed- and rotary-wing aircraft. The USMC's scheme of deployment demanded the availability within the theatre of a complete Marine Expeditionary Force (MEF – one marine division and one marine air wing) within 10 days of the deployment order. The deployment was facilitated by the fact that a move into the Middle East region was one of the standard scenarios around which the USA's Central Command had been planned, so pre-positioned supply ships (carrying war stocks for 30 days) were available at Diego Garcia in the Indian Ocean and arrived in Saudi Arabia on 15 August. There followed two aviation logistic support ships with the equipment and spares to permit the local maintenance of USMC aircraft. Thus it was feasible for the relevant USMC personnel to be flown in direct from the USA by C-5 and C-141 transport aircraft of

the USAF to link up with their equipment at Al Jubail. The first fixed-wing aircraft to arrive to support I MEF were four squadrons of F/A-18 Hornet multi-role aircraft and two squadrons of AV-8B Harrier II STOVL close-support aircraft, which flew direct to Saudi Arabia with inflight refuelling.

When on 8 November 1990 President Bush ordered a major increase in the US strength facing Iraq, opening the way for offensive rather than defensive operations, the I MEF's air strength was boosted to 560 fixed- and rotary-wing aircraft, additional personnel strength being provided by the mobilisation of many thousands of the 4th Marine Air Wing's (MAW) reservists, who were flown into Saudi Arabia to boost the 3rd MAW.

When the coalition launched its initial air offensive against Iraq in January 1991, MAG 11 had six squadrons of F/A-18s (84 machines), two squadrons of Grumman A-6E Intruder attack aircraft (20 machines), one squadron of Grumman EA-6B Prowler electronic warfare aircraft (12 machines) and 15 KC-130 Hercules inflight refuelling tankers. Other air assets available to I MEF at this time included about 60 AV-8Bs and 20 OV-10s in the hands of MAG 11, and 182 assorted helicopters were in the hands of MAG 16 and MAG 26, which was the most recently arrived unit. Another 167 aircraft (141 helicopters and 26 AV-8B) were based on amphibious warfare vessels operating in the Persian Gulf and thus available to the 4th and 5th MEBs as well as the 13th Marine Expeditionary Unit (Special Operations Capable).

The USMC's effort was initially undertaken in support of the I MEF, which comprised the 1st, 4th and 7th Marine Expeditionary Brigades from Kaneohe Bay in Hawaii, Camp Lejeune in North Carolina and Twentynine Palms in California respectively. The 4th MEB was transported by sea to Saudi Arabia during August, but the other two brigades were moved by aircraft of the MAC soon after the Iraqi seizure of Kuwait. These three brigades were the first of an initial 40,000 Marines in the theatre. Once the I MEF had established itself, the Marine Corps began to move in the II MEF, which included the 5th MEB from Camp Pendleton, California. The US Navy's Military Sealift Command was

Attack missions in modern air warfare generally involve a number of different aircraft types to provide comprehensive offensive and defensive capability. A package of attack aircraft, typically Grumman A-6 Intruders and Vought A-7 Corsair IIs, might be escorted and supported by McDonnell Douglas F/A-18 Hornet fighters, defence-suppression machines carrying AGM-88 HARM weapons, and Grumman EA-6B Prowler electronic warfare aircraft of the type seen here. These are machines of the US Marine Corps' VMAQ-2 squadron

Close air support for the ground forces of the US Marine Corps was provided by the McDonnell Douglas/BAe AV-8B Harrier II, a STOVL aircraft able to operate from ships offshore or beach-head airstrips immediately behind the front line

As an armourer checks the loading of 'iron' bombs on the underwing hardpoints of this Grumman A-6E Intruder of the US Marine Corps' VMA(AW)-533 Squadron, the pilot undertakes his walk-round check of the aeroplane before entering the cockpit

responsible for delivering the bulk of the USMC's heavy equipment, including armoured fighting vehicles and helicopters, many of these items coming ashore at the Saudi Arabian port of Al Jubail.

To support this growing force, which could be used in standard land warfare or alternatively for a possible amphibious landing in Kuwait, the USMC called on more than 300 fixed- and rotary-wing aircraft from the 1st and 2nd MAWs allocated to the Fleet Marine Forces in the Pacific and the Atlantic respectively, and also from the 1st Marine Brigade in Hawaii. This concentration of force allowed the basing of seven F/A-18 squadrons at Sheikh Isa for the fighter and attack roles, four McDonnell Douglas/BAe AV-8B Harrier II STOVL close-support aircraft at Al Jubail, two A-6E and one EA-6B squadrons at Sheikh Isa, and two Rockwell OV-10A/D Bronco squadrons at Al Jubail. These 16 squadrons would be primarily responsible for the direct support of USMC operations by fixed-wing aircraft.

As with the USAF and US Navy, inflight refuelling capability was vitally important to the USMC's overall scheme of air operations, and for this task three regular and two reserve marine aerial refuelling transport squadrons (VMGRs) supported the deployment of the USMC's fighter and attack squadrons to the theatre, where some tankers then remained for continued service in the tanker role. The KC-130F/R/T variants of the Hercules transport from the VMGR-234, VMGR-252, VMGR-352 and VMGR-452 squadrons, normally based at the Marine Corps Air Station (MCAS) Glenview in Illinois, MCAS Cherry Point in North Carolina, MCAS El Toro in California and Stewart ANGB in New York respectively, were located at Bahrain during 'Desert Shield'.

The USMC relied on four types of helicopter for its rotary-wing capability, and all of these were deployed to the theatre. To provide close air support there was the Bell AH-1W SuperCobra gunship. This type was flown by the HMLA-367 squadron from MCAS Futenma on Okinawa as well as by the HMLA-267, HMLA-269 and HMLA-369 squadrons from MCAS Camp Pendleton, which were transported to the Middle East by ship, together with their supporting Bell UH-1N 'Huey' helicopters. Several squadrons of CH-46E Sea Knight twin-rotor medium transport helicopters were also delivered by ship, these including the HMM-161 squadron from MCAS Tustin, California, HMM-263 and HMM-265 squadrons from MCAS New River, and HMM-165 squadron from MCAS Kaneohe Bay, Hawaii. Heavy transport, including that of men, vehicles and artillery, was the responsibility of the CH-53D twin-engined and CH-53E three-engined versions of the Sikorsky Sea Stallion: these were operated by several units including HMH-461 squadron from MCAS New River, North Carolina, and HMH-462, HMH-465 and HMH-466 squadrons from MCAS Tustin.

A number of these fixed- and rotary-wing squadrons were brought into the theatre by ship, many by a variety of US Navy assault carriers, as the units had been embarked on board these vessels for six-month cruises in the Mediterranean and Pacific before the start of 'Desert Shield'. Among these ships was the USS *Saipan,* a helicopter assault ship carrying the 22nd Marine Expeditionary Unit as well as its air element, the CH-46E helicopters of Marine Medium Helicopter Squadron (Composite) 261 from MCAS New River. HMH(C)-261 was bolstered before the sailing of the *Saipan* by AH-1 and CH-53 helicopters from other squadrons as well as by a small number of AV-8B fixed-wing aircraft from the

Men of one of the US Marine Corps' marine expeditionary brigades rush forward with BGM-71 TOW reload missiles for a Bell AH-1W SuperCobra helicopter waiting on a forward landing strip in the desert with its rotors turning *(DoD via Robert F Dorr)*

VMA-223 squadron. Three other assault ships that sailed from the USA on 13 August for the waters around the Arabian peninsula were the USS *Iwo Jima,* the USS *Guam* and the USS *Nassau.*

US ARMY

By contrast with the fixed- and rotary-wing aircraft of the USMC, intended for service ashore or afloat, the machines of the US Army were intended solely for land-based deployment and were all helicopters. Although the US Navy and USMC also operated large numbers of helicopters, these numbers were small by comparison with the rotary-wing air strength of the US Army built up in Saudi Arabia during 'Desert Shield'.

US Army helicopters arrived in a steady stream at Dhahran from 8 August on board C-5 Galaxy heavy transports of the USAF, and eventually reached a total of some 1,000 machines for service within the US Army's AirLand Battle concept. This called for a close integration of ground forces and helicopters at all operational levels to facilitate deep and rapid penetrations of the enemy's front, leading to the isolation and destruction of major elements of the enemy's forces.

By 1990 each divison of the US Army contained an organic combat aviation brigade, while each corps had their own organic combat aviation brigades (including two battalions of McDonnell Douglas AH-64 Apache anti-tank helicopters) to provide the capacity for deep strikes at the enemy's rear areas. Also available to the US Army was the 101st Airborne Division (Air Assault), a formation specially trained and equipped for helicopter-delivered and helicopter-supported strategic roles deep in the enemy's rear.

In the course of August and September 1990 the US Army moved six aviation brigades, as well as many smaller support helicopter units, into Saudi Arabia. The first to arrive were the McDonnell Douglas MH-6 and Sikorsky MH-60 machines of the 160th Special Operations Aviation Brigade of the Special Operations Command. At this time the US Army was worried by the notional superiority of the Iraqi armoured forces, equipped with Soviet-supplied modern main battle tanks, that might drive into Saudi Arabia. Therefore, considerable importance was attached to the early delivery of anti-tank helicopter forces.

The first types to arrive in quantity were the McDonnell Douglas AH-64A Apache, Sikorsky UH-60A Black Hawk and Bell OH-58D Kiowa machines that were moved by air for the 82nd Airborne Division, whose 1st Brigade was the first US Army unit to reach Saudi Arabia. This initial wave of deliveries was soon complemented by a flow of similar helicopters to support the arrival of further land forces in the form of the 101st Airborne Division from Fort Campbell, Kentucky, the 1st Infantry Division from Fort Riley, Kansas, and several Army Reserve units. The first base

The two-man crew of a McDonnell Douglas AH-64A Apache anti-tank helicopter prepare to fire up the helicopter's two turboshaft engines and complete final decks before lift-off from a Saudi Arabian base

in Saudi Arabia to witness the build-up of significant US Army aviation assets was Dhahran, which from the beginning of 'Desert Shield' saw the arrival of AH-64A attack and UH-60A transport helicopters of both the 82nd and 101st Airborne Divisions as well as the latter's Boeing CH-47D heavy transport, OH-58C/D scout and EH-60C electronic warfare machines.

The 'Cold War' between the two superpower blocs had recently come to an end with the effective collapse of the USSR. This lowered the level of armed tension in Europe, which had always been seen as the probable main theatre for land warfare between the NATO and Warsaw Pact blocs, and made it possible for the US Army to divert many of its helicopter assets from Germany to Saudi Arabia. This resulted in the allocation of 55 helicopters of 2nd ACR at Feucht, including AH-1F, UH-60A and OH-58C machines, for air transport from Wiesbaden, to which the helicopters flew on 15 November. UH-60A helicopters of the 158th Aviation Regiment and the AH-64A and OH-58C machines of 6th ACR, all stationed at Wiesbaden, also left for Saudi Arabia by November. The OH-58D helicopters of the 158th Aviation Regiment from Bonames, together with about 12 UH-60A machines of sundry medical companies and two C-12C fixed-wing transport aircraft of the 207th Aviation Company, also reached Saudi Arabia by the end of 1990.

Other helicopters of the US Army in Europe were flown to Valkenburg AB in the Netherlands for partial dismantling before being moved to Rotterdam, from where they were shipped to Saudi Arabia. The first of these, on 21 November, were 34 UH-1H, 13 OH-58D and three UH-60A machines of the 159th Aviation Regiment. The process lasted into the first week of December and saw the movement of several hundreds of UH-1H, CH-47D, OH-58, UH-60A, AH-1F, AH-64A and EH-60C helicopters from a large number of units including the 1st and 227th Aviation Regiments at Ansbach and Hanau respectively.

The US forces pay considerable attention to the rapid evacuation of wounded personnel to high-grade medical facilities. In the war against Iraq, this 'dust-off' role was undertaken for the US Army by specially equipped Sikorsky UH-60V Black Hawk helicopters

OPERATION 'DESERT STORM'

On 15 January 1991, the deadline imposed by the United Nations for Iraq to have completed the evacuation of her forces from Kuwait expired. Under the leadership of Saddam Hussein, Iraq had made no effort to comply, and indeed had continued to strengthen her defences in Kuwait and southern Iraq with a mass of fixed fortifications and oil-filled ditches behind which lurked a large and possibly dangerous army with heavy concentrations of armour, artillery and missiles.

The forces of the coalition did not respond immediately, but preparations were almost complete for offensive action, in which a major air campaign would be waged to disable the Iraqi forces and Iraq's command, communications, transport and industrial capabilities. Only after this had been acheived would the ground forces be committed in what it was hoped would be a short campaign to complete the crushing of the Iraqi forces and thus free Kuwait.

At 02.35 on 17 January the air offensive may be said to have got fully under way, with a single 907 kg (2,000 lb) 'Paveway' laser-guided bomb, which struck its target, the AT&T communications building in Baghdad, the Iraqi capital, with devastating accuracy. The weapon had been dropped by an F-117A 'stealth' attack aircraft cruising over Baghdad at only a few thousand feet, wholly undetected by the radars of the Iraqi air-defence system. This was just the first move in a concerted effort spearheaded by a force of F-117As, initially aided by the street lighting of Baghdad. Saddam had not ordered these lights to be turned off, believing that the coalition forces would not dare to attack. The Iraqi dictator clearly believed his forces to be a match for, if not better than, those of the weak Western nations that were the backbone of the coalition.

Whereas aircraft such as the EF-111A and, to a lesser extent, the EA-6B Prowler concentrated on the electronic suppression of Iraq's air-defence capability, a more aggressive role was played by the McDonnell Douglas F-4G 'Wild Weasel'. This used its APR-38 system to detect Iraqi radar emissions and then went for the 'hard' kill of the radar system with the AGM-88 HARM weapon

The 'Desert Storm' campaign was the first in which women saw considerable service as fully integrated members of the armed forces undertaking many roles previously reserved for men

The Panavia Tornado GR 1 aircraft of the Royal Air Force initially operated over Iraq at very low level in a tactic designed originally for use against any Soviet-led attacks on western Europe. However, they later switched to higher-level attacks (Crown Copyright (RAF) via MARS)

Overall, the coalition governments had no fear that their forces would fail to win a crushing victory over Iraq. What was far more problematic was obtaining this military victory without delay and with minimum losses – especially of personnel – thus securing victory in the court of world opinion. It was for this reason that a major emphasis was put on the use of precision-guided weapons. In purely military terms these offered efficiency and economy, and in public relations terms they offered the maximum destruction of specifically military targets with the minimum 'collateral damage' to civilian installations and, more importantly but sometimes unsuccessfully, the civilian population. From the beginning of the campaign the coalition's public relations machinery was able to show that precision-guided munitions were providing just this result, with imagery from attacking aircraft showing guided weapons impacting right on their targets. This trend was confirmed by Western reporters who, before their expulsion from Iraq, were able to show that the conventional warheads of the coalition forces' guided weapons (guided bombs, air-to-surface missiles and, most impressively of all, long-range cruise missiles fired from American warships several hundreds of miles distant from their targets) were causing enormous physical destruction but only a very limited number of civilian casualties.

It was more difficult to judge precisely what strategy Iraq would employ to check the coalition's air onslaught as it would want to buy time for the weight of world opinion to veer from an anti-Iraqi to an anti-coalition angle, and to engineer a situation that might split the fragile unity of the coalition. In the first three or four days of air operations, the Iraqi air force tried to rise to the challenge but was overwhelmed by the coalition's aircraft in the air, and although this was no surprise to analysts who had frequently commented on the poor showing of the Iraqi air force in the 1980-88 war with Iran, it led to the belief in some quarters that the Iraqis were deliberately saving their air force for a decisive intervention once the coalition's armies had been committed.

At the same time it became clear that another plank of Iraq's strategy was an attempt to split the coalition by the use of 'Scud' surface-to-surface ballistic missiles, which could be armed with the biological or chemical warheads that Iraq was known to have developed. The 'Scud' missiles were fired mainly at Riyadh and Dhahran in Saudi Arabia, and at Tel Aviv in Israel. The object of attacks on the former was to persuade the Saudi government that the dangers involved in hosting the coalition forces were too high. The attacks on Tel Aviv were designed to trigger an Israeli armed reaction that would cause Arab nations to disengage from the coalition for pan-Arab reasons. Urged strongly by the Americans, who quickly supplied batteries of the Patriot surface-to-air missiles that were the only possible means of destroying 'Scud' missiles in the air, the Israelis refused to be drawn into military action and thereby reduced the strains on the coalition's continued unity.

Under overall control of the USAF, which was the largest single element in the theatre, the strategy adopted by the UN-mandated coalition was to rip apart the Iraqi command and control system, and at the same time to cut the physical communications between Iraq proper and her forces of occupation in Kuwait. Key targets in this initial phase of the offensive were the Republican Guard formations

A Grumman F-14A Tomcat fighter of the US Navy fires a spread of flares at it climbs over Iraqi territory, the flares being designed to decoy IR-guided missiles that would otherwise home on the fighter's hot exhausts

concentrated along the border between Iraq and Kuwait. An elite force offering personal loyalty to Saddam Hussein and operating the best equipment available to the Iraqi ground forces, the Republican Guard was generally considered to be the most capable military force in Iraqi service. Fielding a higher proportion of armoured fighting vehicles and both armoured and unarmoured transport than the ordinary formations of the Iraqi army, the Republican Guard constituted a highly mobile reserve that was well positioned to intervene at any point that the coalition forces might select for their ground offensive. Therefore, the Republican Guard became the immediate target for heavy carpet-bombing by B-52 heavy bombers delivering large numbers of conventional bombs.

The coalition air forces dropped some 18,000 tonnes of bombs in the first five hours of their offensive, and in the course of the first day of operations some 655 coalition aircraft completed 1,332 sorties against communication centres and 95 airfields (35 of them major centres of Iraqi air activity and the other 60 of lesser significance). The coalition forces claimed that about 80 per cent of their aircraft found and attacked their targets. The Iraqis said that they had brought down 60 aircraft, but in fact only three coalition aircraft failed to return safely, although a larger number were damaged. As the reports of coalition airmen were assessed, it became clear that Iraqi fighters that did rise from their runways did so to

Captain Steve Tate, of the 71st Fighter Squadron within the USAF's 1st Tactical Fighter Wing, scored the coalition's first air victory on 17 January 1991, when he downed an Iraqi Mirage F1EQ with an AIM-7 Sparrow from his McDonnell Douglas F-15C Eagle

escape to the north rather than tackle the coalition's air armada. There was, therefore, little opportunity for air combat but Captain Steve Tate of the USAF did claim a Mirage F1EQ brought down over the outer parts of Baghdad by an AIM-7 Sparrow missile from his F-15 Eagle air-superiority fighter.

Air elements of all four of the American armed forces were heavily involved in the campaign right from its beginning. The US Marine Corps' contribution began with

AH-1W SuperCobra attack helicopters attacking Iraqi artillery batteries, whose personnel ignited the Rad al Khafji oil refinery, just inside Saudi Arabia, on the first day of active operations. The efforts of the attack helicopters paved the way for further attacks by AV-8B Harrier II close-support aircraft operating from land bases.

The US Navy also made its strength tell, the aircraft of each aircraft carrier contributing some 150 sorties per day when they were within range of worthwhile targets. Deployed in the Red Sea were the carriers *Saratoga*, *John F. Kennedy*, *Theodore Roosevelt* and *America*, while in the Persian Gulf and Arabian Sea were the *Midway* and *Ranger*. The naval aircraft most heavily involved in these first stages of the coalition's air offensive were the A-6E Intruder attack and F/A-18 Hornet dual-role fighter/attack machines, with cover provided by the F-14A Tomcat air-superiority fighter and the EA-6B Prowler electronic warfare machine. It was the Prowler that should be credited with the first operations against Iraq, for on 16 January these aircraft started an intensive programme to degrade Iraq's electronic communications network.

An important missile that was rushed into early service for the start of the coalition's campaign was the AGM-84E SLAM, which was the Stand-off Land Attack Missile development of the AGM-84 Harpoon anti-ship missile. The A-6E could carry four of these missiles, and one such aircraft fired two against a hydro-electric plant, with highly effective results: controlled from an A-7E Corsair II, the second of the missiles was guided straight into the hole made by the first, which had been fired two minutes earlier. The efforts of the US Navy A-6E and F/A-18 aircraft were complemented by those of the US Marine Corps, which were land-based at Muharraq on the island state of Bahrain.

An intensive rate of operations was maintained right through the first seven days of the campaign, and although returning pilots brought back telling accounts and strike photographs suggesting a high level of damage to Iraq's infrastructure and her forces, high-level cloud prevented confirmation by reconnaissance imagery from satellites or U-2R/TR-1A aircraft. The highest number of sorties was flown by the USAF, which directed many 'packages' of attack aircraft (generally escorted by F-4G 'Wild Weasel' armed aircraft) to detect and destroy Iraqi air-defence radar sites. EF-111A unarmed aircraft used their powerful onboard systems to find and jam the radar equipment of other air-defence sites. The

The US Navy's first aerial victory of 'Desert Storm' was gained on 17 January 1991 by Lieutenant Commander Mark Fox of the VFA-81 squadron operating from the USS *Saratoga*. Flying a McDonnell Douglas F/A-18C Hornet, Fox brought down a Mikoyan-Gurevich MiG-21 with the unusual combination of one AIM-9 Sidewinder short-range AAM and one AIM-7 Sparrow medium-range AAM. The Sidewinder hit first and the Sparrow then flew into the fireball. Fox's wingman, Lieutenant Nick Mongillo, destroyed another MiG-21 with a Sparrow shot

two most important USAF types for attacks on Iraqi targets were the F-16 Fighting Falcon tactical fighter and the A-10A Thunderbolt II anti-tank and close-support aircraft, each of which could carry a large and widely assorted load of external ordnance, both 'dumb' and 'smart', for attacks against a wide variety of targets.

The work of these tactical aircraft was greatly aided by the availability of both E-8A J-STARS prototypes; types not scheduled to enter service until later in the decade. The E-8A carried a large SLAR (Side-Looking Airborne Radar) in a 'canoe' fairing below the forward part of the fuselage, and with the aid of an advanced operating system this allowed the operators in the fuselage of the converted Boeing 707 transport to 'see' small targets, both moving and stationary, at long slant ranges even in the difficult situation of 'looking' into ground clutter. Such was the capability of the system that operators could locate targets as small as a 'Scud' launch vehicle at a range of some 160 km (100 miles). The E-8A was also fitted with data-link and control systems that allowed real-time transfer of the data to other aircraft and ground stations, and this allowed the rapid engagement and destruction of what might otherwise have been targets too fleeting for realistic engagement.

Another type based on the frame of the Boeing 707 transport was the E-3 Sentry, the airborne warning and control system aeroplane operated by both the USAF and the Royal Saudi Air Force. Orbiting at high altitude but well behind the front line on long-endurance missions, these aircraft used their powerful radars and advanced computer systems to direct and co-ordinate all coalition air activities within a radius of 400 km (250 miles).

The first two days of the campaign were waged by aircraft operating from below Iraq's southern border, but on 19 January another front became active as aircraft based at Incirlik in south-central Turkey entered

In the air, coalition air activities were carefully co-ordinated by the highly trained crews of Boeing E-3B/C Sentry airborne warning and control system aircraft of the 552nd Airborne Warning and Command Wing of the USAF's Tactical air Command normally based at Tinker Air Force Base, Oklahoma

Manned by very highly trained personnel of the USAF's Electronic Security Command, the EC-130H 'Compass Call' version of the C-130 Hercules tactical transport undertook long-duration patrols on the edge of Iraqi airspace to jam and confuse Iraqi radio communications

the fray from a base north of Iraq. Incirlik was temporary home to a comparatively small but well-balanced force of tactical aircraft, and attack packages from this base generally comprised F-111E and F-16 aircraft operating on the basis of reconnaissance information provided by RF-4C machines and protected by F-15 fighters as well as the electronic ministration of EF-111A machines.

Incirlik was also the base from which EC-130H jammer aircraft flew sorties to degrade if not 'blind' radar and communication systems not physically destroyed by bombs and anti-radar missiles. The first day of the coalition's air campaign was characterised by a major Iraqi effort to use its large numbers of ground-based radars to find the targets that would then, in theory, be destroyed by surface-to-air missiles and anti-aircraft artillery. So successful were the coalition's anti-radar efforts, however, that almost immediately there were virtually no surviving Iraqi radars or, perhaps, any which were prepared to reveal their position by emitting. Tacit confirmation of this was provided by the Iraqis' claims for the number of coalition aircraft shot down: after announcing that her forces had shot down 170 aircraft (only 14 had in fact been lost) during the first four days of the coalition offensive, Iraq thereafter claimed almost no more victories despite the fact that very substantial numbers of aircraft continued to operate in the skies over the country.

In the first week of their offensive, the coalition air forces flew more than 12,000 sorties and were able to claim that their work was continuing to schedule despite unfavourable weather conditions. On the following day (24 January) the weather improved considerably, and the coalition air

Generally known as the 'Spark Vark' or 'Electric Fox', the Grumman-developed EF-111A version of the F-111 interdictor was one of the US Air Force's most important aircraft of the war: the type carried no weapons, but as an electronic warfare type was vital for the protection of packages of attack aircraft

forces flew no fewer than 3,000 sorties. By this time the coalition's strategic concept had been revised to place greater emphasis on the destruction of infrastructure targets such as electricity-generation plants and oil refineries as well as the sites at which chemical warfare weapons were likely to be produced and stored. The coalition also claimed that Iraq's nuclear weapon development capability had been wholly destroyed.

In the first seven days of operations, some 16 per cent of the coalition's air effort was undertaken by non-American air units, the primary contributions coming (not in order of magnitude) from the air components of Canada, France, Italy, Kuwait, Saudi Arabia and the UK. Of these the country that made the single greatest contribution was the UK, whose Tornado GR 1 force suffered comparatively heavy losses while undertaking attacks on Iraqi airfields with JP233 submunitions dispensers at night and at heights of little more than 60 m (200 ft). The attacks certainly inflicted damage on the airfields, but the fact that the aircraft had to cross strongly defended areas meant that they faced the attentions of carefully sited anti-aircraft guns and surface-to-air missiles, and had also to manoeuvre at very low altitude, SAMs and low-level manoeuvring each accounting for two Tornados. The British losses with this tactic, which had been designed for use against Soviet airfields in the altogether different terrain of Europe, were 26 per cent of the coalition's total losses for the period between 17 and 23 January. Altogether five aircraft were lost out of a total strength of 42 machines of this type.

The British started to revise their tactics on 20 January, the low-level attacks with submunition dispensers giving way to medium-altitude attacks at up to 7,620 m (25,000 ft) with each aircraft carrying eight 454 kg (1,000 lb) bombs. This reflected the fact that low-level missions were no longer required as a means of entering defended airspace under the radar net (which had ceased to exist in any useful form). It did reduce the Tornado GR 1's loss rate, but also emphasised the fact that significant results were difficult to obtain with free-fall 'dumb' bombs. At this time the Tornado GR 1 force were incapable of delivering 'smart' ordnance, so on 26 January eight Buccaneer S 2B aircraft of No 12 Squadron arrived in the theatre to provide them with support. The Buccaneer's AVQ-23 'Pave Spike' laser-designation system was used to 'illuminate' targets that

The BAe Buccaneer S 2B was in the last stages of its service life with the Royal Air Force when its capabilities were demanded in Saudi Arabia to provide laser illumination for the laser-guided bombs carried by other aircraft. Seen in the course of ground tests at Muharraq, this Buccaneer carries four stores under its wing: from left to right these are ALQ-101(V)10 radar jammer, a slipper fuel tank, the AVQ-23E 'Pave Spike' laser pod (with its optics covered) and AIM-9L Sidewinder short-range AAMs for self-protection

The BAe Buccaneer S 2B aircraft provided by Nos 12 and 208 Squadrons as well as No 237 Operational Conversion Unit were initially deployed to use their AVQ-23E 'Pave Spike' laser designating pods to 'illuminate' targets for the laser-guided bombs dropped by Tornado GR 1 aircraft, but from 21 February themselves dropped 48 such bombs *(Crown Copyright (RAF) via MARS)*

could then be attacked with pinpoint accuracy by the laser-guided bombs which became increasingly the standard weapons of the Tornado GR 1 force.

By this time there was little need for further attacks on Iraqi airfields, which had virtually all been incapacitated or deserted by the surviving aircraft that should have been based on them, and the coalition moved towards destroying the Iraqi land forces that might impede the eventual advance of the coalition's army formations. During the night of 25/26 January, for instance, Tornado GR 1s made three attacks on Republican Guard positions and supply dumps. their destruction of a fuel and ammunition dump produced a fireball that could be seen by the pilots of aircraft some 320 km (200 miles) away.

After an inauspicious start, which also included the loss of similar Italian and Saudi Arabian aircraft, the Tornado GR 1 began to reveal its true capabilities. These were further enhanced in theory by the advent of the ALARM anti-radar missile. Another 'plus' for the Tornado forces was the success of the Tornado GR 1A reconnaissance model, a development of the Tornado GR 1 with a highly capable IR system that provided good imagery under virtually all conditions including those that prevented the

This Panavia Tornado F 3 air-superiority fighter of No 11 (Composite) Squadron reveals the standard external load of four Sky Flash 90 medium-range AAMs under the fuselage, and two drop tanks and two or four AIM-9M Sidewinder short-range AAMs under the wing *(Ian Black)*

use of aircraft with optical imaging systems. On 18 January, for instance, a pair of Tornado GR 1A aircraft captured on IR video a mobile 'Scud' launcher of the type that was being used for the bombardment of Israel.

Given the unwillingness or, more realistically, the inability of the Iraqi air force to fly missions against the coalition base areas, the Tornado F 3 air-defence fighters of the RAF and the Royal Saudi Air Force had little or no opportunity for action, although some of the British aircraft were used for combat air patrols. One opportunity did seem to beckon on 18 January, when a Tornado F 3 combat air patrol (CAP) was vectored into an area in which Iraqi fighters were detected approaching A-10A Thunderbolt IIs, but the Iraqis decamped before the British fighters could arrive.

As the weight of the offensive made itself felt, the coalition's CAPs were pushed forward over the southern part of Iraq, but still the British fighter pilots found no 'trade'. However, the Saudi Arabians had better luck when Captain Ayedh of No 13 Squadron in an F-15C Eagle gained the war's first double victory after he was vectored into an interception that resulted in the destruction of two Mirage F1s. These were escorting a Mirage F1EQ on a mission, immediately aborted, to fire an Exocet missile at coalition warships operating in the northern part of the Persian Gulf.

During the build-up of the coalition force the British inflight refuelling capability had rested with VC10 and Victor aircraft, which were reinforced, as operations began, by Tristars. Although far fewer in overall number than the KC-10 and KC-135 tanker force operated by the USAF, the British tankers were soon an intrinsic part of the coalition air effort as they topped up the fuel of attack aircraft outbound for Iraq or inbound after a sortie with fuel low as a result of range or damage. The British tankers supplied a wide range of aircraft including, at times, US Navy types such as the F-14A Tomcat and EA-6B Prowler.

Other coalition aircraft involved in operations from the first day of the offensive were the A-4KU attack aircraft of the Free Kuwait Air Force and the CF-18 Hornet dual-role aircraft of the Canadian Armed Forces. A militarily modest but politically significant further addition came on 22 January, when Qatar committed its small Mirage F1 force to the war despite the fact that the Iraqis were flying a variant of the same basic aircraft, therefore risking misidentification. Further Arab commitment to the war came on 25 January when the F-16 tactical aircraft of Bahrain entered combat, defensive operations on the first day turning to offensive operations the next.

Seated on a zero/zero ejection seat with the screen of the HUD in his forward line of sight, the pilot of this McDonnell Douglas F-15C air-superiority fighter has excellent all-round fields of vision through the carefully designed canopy

The position of the French air force component in Saudi Arabia was complicated by the fact that the French defence minister, a supporter of Iraq, ordered that no missions should be flown against Iraq. Therefore, the French force of Jaguar A attack aircraft was restricted to sorties against the Iraqi positions in Kuwait until 24 January, when the minister was overruled by President Mitterrand and the remit of the French squadrons was expanded to include Iraq. The French aircraft then struck at the Republican Guards, whose formations were attacked with free-fall bombs while fixed targets such as bunkers used as command centres or ammunition stores were tackled successfully with AS.30L laser-guided missiles. The equivalent British force, flying the Jaguar GR 1, had been in operation since 17 January against targets in Iraq as well as Kuwait. The British generally operated by day, and used 454 kg (1,000 lb) free-fall bombs as well as 70 mm (2.75 in) air-to-surface unguided rockets on targets that included surface-to-air missile sites and, on 26 January, a Kuwaiti coastal site equipped with Chinese CSS-N-1 'Silkworm' anti-ship missiles.

As the offensive gathered pace and momentum, helicopter forces began to play an increasingly significant part. SH-60B Seahawks of the US Navy were used to deploy frogmen tasked with the deactivation of Iraqi floating mines that prejudiced naval operations, real and threatened, in the northern waters of the Persian Gulf, while Lynx helicopters embarked on various British warships were involved in the hunting and destruction of Iraqi fast attack craft with Sea Skua light anti-ship missiles. Two of the helicopters, in this instance from HMS *Gloucester*, were also involved in the 19 January seizure of nine maritime oil platforms held by the Iraqis. Four days later one of the *Gloucester*'s helicopters discovered that the Iraqis were using an oil tanker off Iraq's short coastline as an early warning post, and the report of this fact led to the destruction of the tanker by American aircraft. On the next day the Lynx from HMS *Cardiff* located an Iraqi

Fitted with a centreline drop tank and, under the wing, outboard AAMs and inboard 'iron' bombs, this Jaguar A of the French air force is taking off with full afterburner for an attack mission

Carrying two examples each of the Super 530 medium- and Magic short-range AAMs under its wing, this aircraft preparing to take-off on a combat air patrol is a Dassault Mirage 2000C of the French air force's EC 5 unit

The most important anti-tank helicopter fielded by the British army was the Westland Lynx AH 7, seen here in flight with four of its eight BGM-71 TOW heavyweight anti-tank missiles visible. Guidance was provided by means of the M65 stabilised sight in the roof of the cockpit

minesweeper and was about to attack with a Sea Skua missile when the effort was called off in favour of an attempt to seize the vessel with a boarding party. This was achieved with the aid of a Lynx from HMS *London*, and led to the first liberation of Kuwaiti territory when the tiny island of Qaruh was captured without loss from its Iraqi garrison.

In overall terms, the first days of the coalition air offensive were an unmitigated disaster for Iraq, which suffered enormous physical damage and had all her forces, land, sea and air, devastated by virtually unmolested coalition air power. The coalition air arms were able to operate where and when they wanted without fear of Iraqi air force intervention, for it had become clear that such Iraqi aircraft as survived were not prepared to venture into the air even where an intact runway was still available. Even so, some in the coalition camp still expressed a fear that the Iraqi air force was not so much beaten as biding its time, with its air-defence radars switched off and its main strength hidden in well concealed bunkers awaiting the decisive moment, when it would be unleashed against the coalition's ground offensive with chemical weapons.

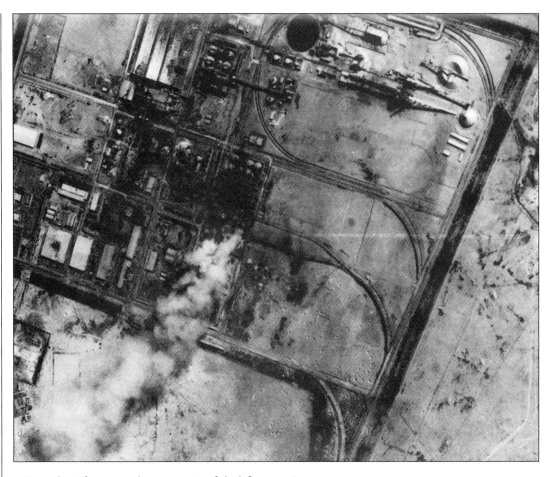

Even the information that many aircraft had flown to Iran was not greeted with unalloyed joy, for while many saw this as tacit evidence of the Iraqi air force's concession of defeat in the air war, others saw it as an Iraqi ploy to preserve at least some of their air strength for future use at a decisive moment. This fear was based on the belief that Iran's professed neutrality might be a sham, for the religious leadership of Iran was known to be at least partially in favour of putting aside the legacy of the two countries' animosity in the 1980-88 war in favour of collaborative action in a jihad (holy war) against the USA and its allies, in particular Israel.

By 27 January the coalition's air forces had lost no aircraft in air combat, while the Iraqi air force had suffered the loss of 22 aircraft in the air and 23 more on the ground, the latter figure including three Tu-16 'Badger' medium bombers as they were preparing to take-off from the air base at Qayyarah West on 23 January. Another highly satisfactory factor for the coalition was that the Iraqi air force's most capable fighter, the MiG-29 'Fulcrum', had been no threat at all, as at least eight had been shot down without loss to the coalition's own fighters. Iraq had claimed the destruction of more than 200 coalition aircraft by its ground-based air defence forces, but the reality was a mere 17 aircraft including nine American machines. This represented a loss rate of only 0.025 per cent for the figure of more than 22,000 sorties that had been undertaken before the end of the campaign's 11th day.

The mass of craters in and around the fertiliser factory at Al Qaim provides telling evidence of the efforts launched by the coalition air forces to destroy key elements of Iraq's economic infrastructure

Although the losses of the coalition air forces were remarkably low, many of their aircraft were damaged, more or less severely, by the vast quantity of missiles and anti-aircraft artillery projectiles the Iraqis lofted into the sky over their country; an example is this McDonnell Douglas F/A-18A Hornet of the VMFA-314 'Black Knights' squadron, a US Marine Corps' unit that had every reason to be glad of the Hornet's very considerable ability to absorb and survive battle damage

Overall the coalition air forces had achieved a very considerable success in the first days of its offensive, and the coalition had every reason to be pleased with progress. The one unfortunate aspect of the war to date had been the rate of Iraqi 'Scud' missile launches. These were not significant in purely military terms, but were a major feature in the public relations war that was in many respects as important as military events as it was the first war conducted in the glare of real-time television coverage from both sides of the line.

By 28 January, the 12th day of the air offensive, the coalition could justifiably claim total air supremacy over Iraq, especially as the Iraqi air force had wherever possible decamped to Iran. By 7 February, the 22nd day of the coalition's offensive, these defections had risen to 137 aircraft including 25 transport machines as well as five MiG-25 'Foxbat', eight MiG-29 'Fulcrum', 24 Mirage F1EQ, virtually all 24 Sukhoi Su-24 'Fencer' and both Adnan AEW machines. Iraq's loss of five MiG-29s,(the best fighter available to her and presumably flown by the Iraqi air force's most privileged, if not best trained, pilots) during the first five days of the conflict must have given a clear pointer of the way things would go if other pilots presented themselves and their aircraft as targets.

A type new in service as the air war against Iraq started was the Panavia Tornado GR 1A reconnaissance aeroplane fitted with a Vinten 4000 horizon-to-horizon IR linescan system and a system for the real-time transfer of data to a ground station. Although there were a number of teething problems, the Tornado GR 1A proved itself useful for hunting the 'Scud' missiles and their launchers on which the Iraqis were largely reliant in their attempts to break up the coalition with attacks on Saudi Arabia and Israel

In these circumstances the three primary types of air-superiority fighter available to the coalition (the F-15 flown by the USAF and Royal Saudi Air Force, the Tornado F 3 operated by the RAF and Royal Saudi Air Force, and the Mirage 2000 manned by the French air force) could be confident that they faced no realistic threat of Iraqi challenge and, with the upper air to themselves, could now with the exception of the Tornado move up to offensive patrols deeper into southern Iraq. Here their most likely prey, detected by E-3 AWACS aircraft that would control the most economical interceptions, were further Iraqi aircraft trying to make the run to Iran. However, during the first week of February AWACS aircraft detected only one flight; a week later, the AWACS aircraft had found no more Iraqi aircraft in the air. This was a portent of the continuing shape of the war, and with the exception of a few helicopter flights no Iraqi aircraft took to the air after that day.

This greatly aided the pace and scale of the coalition air effort, for even unarmed aircraft such as the vital inflight refuelling tankers could be moved north to orbits over the southern part of Iraq, thereby greatly easing the task of mounting attack missions still deeper into Iraq. These attacks were at first targeted primarily against strategic objectives, but from late February the number of such targets left had declined considerably and there were more pressing tactical targets as the coalition moved toward the start of its land offensive. Therefore, the emphasis of the air attacks moved south again, to the Iraqis' land links with Kuwait and the Iraqi border with Saudi Arabia, and then to the men and equipment that were becoming increasingly isolated in Kuwait and southern Iraq. Attacks on these targets alone would have allowed the Iraqis to deduce the nature of the forthcoming land war, however, and for this reason attacks were also made by fixed- and rotary-wing aircraft against Iraq's surviving ships and installations in a largely successful ploy to persuade the Iraqis that the coalition was still planning an amphibious assault on Kuwait – the Iraqis, therefore, kept a considerable garrison there.

Despite the heavy attacks on Iraq's front-line formations in southern Iraq and Kuwait, where their capabilities were very seriously degraded, the coalition air forces also continued their intensive operations against Baghdad and the major concentrations of Republic Guard formations that constituted Iraq's strategic reserve in the south.

The coalition's supposed preparation for an amphibious assault became evident to the Iraqis on 26 January, when RAF Jaguar GR 1 attack aircraft struck at coastal defence missile batteries in Kuwait. This belief was further reinforced in the minds of the Iraqis on 29 January, when Lynx HAS 3 helicopters of the Fleet Air Arm collaborated with A-6E Intruder fixed-wing aircraft of the US Navy and OH-58D helicopters of the US Army and struck at Iraqi patrol craft, sinking five such craft and damaging another 12. The attack was renewed on the following day, claiming six more craft. This fascinating little offensive continued to the end of the month, and resulted in the loss of 46 Iraqi craft. This meant there was no realistic Iraqi naval threat in the northern waters of the Persian Gulf, and as a result even ships as large as the battleship USS *Missouri* could operate in these waters from 4 February. The *Missouri,* therefore, operated off the coast of Kuwait as a floating battery of super-heavy artillery, engaging and destroying land targets with her 406 mm (16 in) main guns.

However it was during this period, when the Lynx helicopters of the Fleet Air Arm seemed rampant in and around the northern end of the Persian Gulf, that the Iraqi forces gained their only tactical success of the entire war. On 29 January an Iraqi force took the town of Khafji, just a few miles into Saudi Arabia, despite intervention by American aircraft (AH-1W SuperCobra and AH-64A Apache helicopters together with

Despite its lack of advanced offensive electronics, the SEPECAT Jaguar GR 1 proved itself an effective, reliable and rugged aircraft in British service. Seen on its way to the target, this machine carries offensive armament in the form of 'Rockeye' anti-tank cluster bombs, defensive armament in the form of AIM-9L Sidewinder short-range AAMs, and defensive electronics in the form of an ALQ-101 jammer pod and a Phimat chaff dispenser pod

AV-8B Harriers and A-10A Thunderbolt IIs) that dealt severely with an Iraqi armoured element supporting the infantry thrust. The Iraqis gained a measure of propaganda success from their seizure of Khafji, but no real military advantage, especially as the men in and around the Saudi Arabian town suffered heavy losses from attacks by AC-130H gunship aircraft of the USAF's 16th Special Operations Squadron, which lost one of its aircraft.

From the last days of January the coalition air forces began a major effort to ensure the total isolation of southern Iraq and Kuwait from the rest of Iraq. This effort concentrated on the destruction of the bridges needed for any significant southward movement of men and, more importantly, armour and artillery. The key weapon in this effort was the laser-guided bomb, and by 30 January the coalition air forces had hit 33 of the 36 strategic bridges over the Tigris and Euphrates rivers downstream of Baghdad, and had inflicted further damage on the bridges of Baghdad itself. The Iraqi forces attempted to restore their links with the south with pontoon bridges, but a regular watch was kept on such efforts, which received devastating air attacks as soon as they were nearly complete. The overall success of this coalition effort is shown by the fact that movement between Baghdad and Kuwait declined by some 90 per cent.

Iraqi airfields were also visited regularly to prevent repairs being undertaken, and by the end of January 38 airfields had been attacked, eight of them being effectively destroyed and the others rendered inoperable for the immediate future. The aircraft that were most significant in this effort were the F-111s of the USAF, and the Tornado interdictors of the British, Italian and Saudi air forces. By early February it had become clear that the Iraqis did not intend to repair the damaged runways, and the coalition changed tack to ensure that no aircraft could be brought back, either from Iran or from concealed accommodation in Iraq, to operate from these air bases after any lightning repairs once the coalition had started its land campaign. The coalition air forces, therefore, began to destroy every one of the Iraqi air force's almost 600 hardened aircraft shelters. This meant that even if aircraft were brought back onto the airfields, they could not be concealed or sheltered, and would be totally exposed to immediate destruction on the ground. By 30 January some 70 hardened aircraft shelters had been destroyed, this figure rising to 345 by 15 February, by which time the onslaught was seen as largely irrelevant and scaled down.

The primary weapon against hardened aircraft shelters was, again, the 'Paveway' series of laser-guided bombs. The USAF used its F-111F aircraft, carrying a centreline 'Pave Tack' laser designation system, to drop 907 kg (2,000 lb) laser-guided bombs, while the RAF used 454 kg (1,000 lb) laser-guided bombs delivered by Tornado GR 1s, each of which generally operated with two or three such weapons. The Tornado GR 1 lacked any inbuilt laser designation system, so four of the aircraft were used as the platforms for the only two available examples of the new TIALD pod, which offered night as well as day capability, and other designation capability was provided by the 'Pave Spike' day-only pods carried by 12 Buccaneer S 2B aircraft specially flown in for the task.

In the absence of any Iraqi opposition there was no operational reason for the Tornados to restrict themselves to nocturnal operations, so the force began day attacks on 2 February. Operating at an altitude of 6,095 m (20,000 ft) or more, the Tornados were effectively invulnerable to the Iraqis' largest-calibre anti-aircraft artillery, radar-laid 100 mm (3.94 in) weapons whose shells were nearing their apogee at that height and therefore moving so slowly that they could virtually be seen and avoided. Even in these circumstances, with no Iraqi intervention at all likely, the Tornados were generally supported by American aircraft. Although they were operating from Tabuk on the western side of Saudi Arabia, the Tornados were often supported and supplemented by F-14A Tomcat fighters and A-6E Intruder attack aircraft from carriers operating in the Red Sea, on the western side of Saudi Arabia. The Intruder was also highly capable in the laser-guided bombing role, for it had its own laser designation system in the TRAM (Target Recognition and Attack Multi-sensor) system in a trainable turret under the nose.

The Iraqi anti-aircraft gunners and surface-to-air missile operators were increasingly reluctant to reveal their positions by activating their weapons' radar systems, for this inevitably invited the retaliation of EA-6B Prowler, F/A-18 Hornet and F-4G 'Wild Weasel' defence-suppression aircraft, which could locate and use an AGM-88 HARM (High-speed Anti-Radiation Missile) to destroy a hostile radar well within the 30 seconds needed for the Iraqi radar to acquire a target and guide a missile onto it.

The coalition air forces stepped up their attacks on Republican Guard formations early in February. The most morale-sapping of the raids were mounted by B-52G Stratofortress heavy bombers operating from comparatively nearby bases in Saudi Arabia and from the island base of Diego Garcia, but also from considerably more distant locations such as

One of the weapons used to very telling effect by the General Dynamics F-111F interdictors of the 48th Tactical Fighter Wing was the GBU-15 glide bomb, which had a range of some 80 km (50 miles) when launched at high altitude. In the nose of the weapon was either a TV seeker for day use or an IR seeker for night and adverse-weather use: the operator in the aircraft locking the missile onto its target after launch then leaving it to complete its autonomous attack

The McDonnell Douglas F/A-18 Hornet carried the AGM-88 HARM weapon for the suppression of Iraq's ground-based air defences. Here armourers load this weapon onto the outer hardpoint under the dual-role fighter's port wing

The F-15E variant of the McDonnell Douglas F-15 Eagle was optimised for the long-range day/night attack role with a large and diverse weapons load that could be delivered with great accuracy

Moron AB in Spain and RAF Fairford in England. Spanish permission for the USAF to mount attacks from Spanish territory was very surprising, as was French authorisation for the USAF to base KC-135 inflight refuelling tankers at Mont-de-Marsan to top up the tanks of bombers on their way to Iraq, with an offensive load typically comprising 51 340 kg (750 lb) M117 bombs internally and externally. By 9 February aircraft of the coalition air forces had dropped some 80,000 tonnes of bombs on Iraq.

Even though the coalition air forces were completing about 2,500 sorties per day, by 8 February it was estimated that the air campaign was some eight days behind schedule. This shortfall was the result largely of adverse weather but also to an extent of the need to divert some 100 to 150 sorties to the difficult task of finding and then attacking the mobile 'Scud' launchers on which Iraq had pinned her hopes of breaking up the coalition. The 'Scud' effort required the extensive use of comparatively scarce reconnaissance assets, and also the mounting of standing patrols of F-15E attack aircraft that could respond immediately to any sighting and prevent the escape of the launcher.

The effort against the 'Scud' launchers also involved ground teams of British and American special forces, who also had a number of other responsibilities. The need to deliver, support and extract these teams required considerable use of helicopters, such as the MH-53J, MH-60J and CH-47 types supported by the MC-130E 'Combat Talon II' and HC-130N/P versions of the Hercules transport, all of which suffered little in the way of losses as there was by now no Iraqi air threat. Among the tasks undertaken by the special forces teams was the rescue of airmen who had come down in Iraqi territory. The activities of the special forces teams were a constant thorn in the side of the Iraqis, as much for psychological as purely military reasons, and further pressure was exerted by the use of psychological warfare aircraft such as the EC-130E(RR) Hercules.

With the date for the coalition's ground offensive approaching, it was essential that the extensive minefields laid by the Iraqis in front of their positions should be neutralised. Among the several methods used for this task, one of the most unusual made its debut on 15 February when C-130 aircraft started to drop 6,804 kg (15,000 lb) 'Daisy Cutter' devices, which detonated the mines within a large radius of their detonation point with the pressure wave of their blast.

Ground and air probes toward the Iraqi front became more frequent

and also more aggressive. The crumbling of Iraqi morale, especially among the unwilling conscripts who constituted the bulk of Iraq's front-line formations, was revealed on 17 February, when two of the US Army's AH-64A attack helicopters returned from a probing flight shepherding some 20 men who had surrendered to the helicopters. During this period the efforts of the coalition air forces moved steadily closer to the front line. B-52 bombers made carpet bombing raids that caused as much psychological as physical damage, while coalition attack aircraft concentrated on the piecemeal destruction of the Iraqis' heavy weapons with attacks on individual tanks and pieces of artillery using precision guided weapons as well as 'dumb' weapons such as bombs (free-fall and retarded), cluster bombs and air-to-surface unguided rockets. So far as the 'smart' ordnance was concerned, the laser-guided bomb again proved invaluable as its lack of a motor made it a cost-effective weapon, but extensive use was also made of air-to-surface missiles such as the AGM-65D version of the Maverick with imaging infra-red guidance by tactical aircraft including the F-15E, F-16 and F-111. These generally launched their attacks soon after the setting of the sun, when metal was still hot but the surrounding sand had cooled, offering a high level of thermal contrast that ensured the most successful

The war with Iraq saw widespread use of American special forces, which were infiltrated and extracted by the Sikorsky MH-60J Pave Hawk, a type making its combat debut with the Special Operations Command. With its armour, armament, special sensors and long-range, the helicopter was also used for combat search-and-rescue missions

The US Navy's counterpart of the MH-60J, the Sikorsky HH-60H, although optimised for combat search and rescue was also used for the support of covert operations

The smallest air-to-surface guided missile used by fixed-wing aircraft in the campaign against Iraq was the AGM-65 Maverick. This example under the port wing of a Fairchild Republic A-10A Thunderbolt II anti-tank and battlefield attack aircraft is an AGM-65A/B with an optronic guidance system, as indicated by the clear window on the nose

use of the missile. Large numbers of armoured fighting vehicles and artillery pieces were destroyed using this tactic, typical nightly success figures being 200 in clear weather and 100 in cloudy weather.

The land campaign was scheduled to start on 24 February, and by the day before the coalition air forces had claimed the destruction of 1,685 tanks (some 60 per cent of Iraq's strength), 925 armoured personnel carriers and 1,485 pieces of artillery. By this time the Iraqi air force and navy had effectively ceased to operationally exist. The coalition effort to secure this ideal position in which to start the land offensive had involved the dropping of 60,000 tonnes of bombs (some 150,000 weapons) in 94,000

Protected against the harsh sunlight of the region but little else, this General Dynamics F-16C Fighting Falcon was a workhorse of the American air effort. Here members of the ground crew bring up a Tactical Munitions Dispenser, a weapon that carried a mix of anti-armour and anti-personnel mines

sorties. Considerable damage had also been inflicted on the Iraqi forces by naval bombardment in the area of Kuwait, by artillery, and by the large-calibre rockets fired from MLRS (Multiple-Launch Rocket System) launchers.

The coalition ground forces started their advance at 04.30 on 24 February under the cover of concentrated air power provided by the coalition air forces' massed attack and close support aircraft as well by the ground forces' own armed helicopters. The Iraqi defence was based largely on the belief that the coalition's primary effort would be made by ground and amphibious forces in and around Kuwait, but in fact the main weight of the coalition offensive had shifted to the west, where major armoured forces plunged though the Iraqi right wing before hooking eastward to cut the Iraqis' lines of communication or, as soon became clear, lines of retreat.

With the coalition's left flank shielded by French troops and Gazelle anti-tank helicopters against the unlikely event of any Iraqi attempt to take the main thrust in flank, the men and machines of the American ground forces swept forward with some 300 CH-47D Chinook heavy lift and AH-64A Apache battlefield helicopters to secure a forward operating base, codenamed Cobra, at Salman airfield, some 80 km (50 miles) inside Iraq. On 24 February the coalition air forces flew more than 3,000 tactical sorties, including 1,300 against targets in Kuwait and 700 more for close air support.

With his forces outflanked, and lacking the matériel and command strengths to provide any kind of counter, Saddam Hussein was faced with the problem of what to do with the surviving elements of his army, around which the coalition's grasp was tightening rapidly as all attempts at movement were instantly checked by the activities of AV-8B Harrier,

The coalition air forces did not have things all their own way, as suggested by the damage to this Grumman A-6E Intruder. Hit by ground fire, the aeroplane returned to its parent carrier with its two crew members unharmed, but was later scrapped

Carrying multi-tube rocket launchers and AGM-114 Hellfire anti-tank missiles in addition to the 30 mm Chain Gun cannon under the fuselage, the McDonnell Douglas AH-64A Apache proved itself wholly the master of Iraqi armoured formations

A-6E Intruder, A-10A Thunderbolt II, AC-130H 'Spectre' and even B-52G aircraft. Saddam proclaimed publicly that his forces had won a great victory but privately ordered all surviving forces to fall back as, when and how they could. The land campaign lasted just 100 hours, and in this time the Iraqi army lost about half of the 42 divisions it had deployed to the theatre. The garrison of Kuwait fled north as best it could, often in plundered Kuwaiti vehicles laden with booty, but the coalition air forces made their northward dash a misery of burned-out vehicles and killed men. After public and private expressions of concern about the loss of Iraqi life, especially after reports of total destruction on a 4.8 km (3 mile) stretch of the main route north from Kuwait, President Bush decided to cut short the offensive.

Almost the final event of the war was the use over Abu Gharb, near Baghdad, of two 2,132 kg (4,700 lb) 'bunker-buster' laser-guided bombs. Hastily created from sections of 203 mm (8 in) gun barrel to provide a casing able to penetrate deep into the earth and even through concrete

Armed with the devastating 30 mm GAU-8/A Avenger rotary cannon in its forward fuselage for tank-killing purposes, the Fairchild Republic A-10A Thunderbolt II is a decisive battlefield aircraft with this and underwing weapons that can include the AGM-65 Maverick air-to-surface missile, multi-tube launchers for air-to-surface unguided rockets, and free-fall stores such as these Mk 20 Rockeye II cluster bombs; each carrying 247 Mk 119 anti-tank bomblets

before detonating, these weapons were dropped by F-111s on an Iraqi high-level command bunker, in which many of Iraq's senior officers are believed to have perished.

The coalition's forces ended their offensive on 28 February. By this time the Iraqis had left Kuwait, whose liberation had been the primary objective of the war. The Iraqi army had suffered an unknown but very large number of casualties as well as the destruction of 3,700 tanks and the capture of 175,000 men. On the other side, the coalition forces had suffered the loss of only 150 personnel killed while completing a total rout of their opponents. There can be no doubt that the small scale of the coalition losses and totally comprehensive success of their ground offensive were the direct results of the coalition's overwhelming air campaign of more than 110,000 sorties.

A scene typical of those faced by coalition ground forces as they moved into Kuwait: before pulling back to avoid being encircled, the Iraqi occupation forces blew up and ignited some 700 oil wells

After the hammering they had received from the air as well as from the coalition's ground forces, very large numbers of Iraqi troops surrendered to the advancing allied divisions, showing relief at their survival rather than despondency at their defeat

APPENDICES

AIR FORCES ORDER OF BATTLE IN THE GULF WAR

**US Air Force
(directly assigned)**

Unit		Aircraft type	Base (home/forward)	Dates in theatre
Air Force Systems Command				
4411th J-STARS Sqn		E-8A	Melbourne, Florida/Riyadh	Jan/Mar
Military Airlift Command				
314th TAW	50th TAS	C-130E	Little Rock AFB, Arkansas/Abu Dhabi Int'l Ap't	Feb/Mar
	61st TAS	C-130E	Incirlik	
317th TAW	?th TAS	C-130E	Pope AFB, North Carolina/Masirah	
			& Thumrait, later forward deployed	
			to Damman/King Fahd Int'l Ap't	
374th TAW	21st TAS	C-130E	Clark AB/Thumrait	Feb/Mar
345th TAS		C-130E	Yokota AB/Thumrait	Feb/Mar
435th TAW	37th TAS	C-130E	Rhein-Main AB/Al Ain	Aug/Mar
463rd TAW	772nd TAS	C-130H	Dyess AFB, Texas/Al Kharj AB	?
	773rd TAS	C-130H	Al Kharj AB	Dec
375th TAW				
1401st MAS	Det 3	C-21A	Barksdale AFB, Louisiana/Riyadh	Aug & Feb/Mar
1401st MAS	Det 4	C-21A	Peterson AFB, Colorado/Riyadh	Mar
1402nd MAS	Det 1	C-21A	Langley AFB, Virginia/Riyadh	Jan/Mar
1402nd MAS	Det 3	C-21A	Maxwell AFB, Alabama/Riyadh	Sep & Feb
1402nd MAS	Det 4	C-21A	Eglin AFB, Florida/Riyadh	Jan
Special Operations Command				
1st SOW				
8th SOS		MC-130E	Hurlburt Field, Florida/Damman/King Fahd Int'l Ap't	Aug/Mar
9th SOS		HC-130N/P	Eglin AFB, Florida/Damman/King Fahd Int'l Ap't	Aug/Mar
16th SOS		AC-130H	Hurlburt Field, Florida/unrevealed	Sep/Mar
20th SOS		MH-53J	Hurlburt Field, Florida/unrevealed	Nov/Mar
55th SOS		MH-60G	Eglin AFB, Florida/unrevealed	Nov/Mar
39th SOW				
21st SOS		MH-53J	RAF Woodbridge/Incirlik & Batman AB	Jan/Mar
67th SOS		HC-130N/P	RAF Woodbridge/Incirlik & Batman AB	Jan/Mar
Strategic Air Command (reconnaissance & bomber aircraft)				
9th SRW				
99th SRS		TR-1A/U-2R	Beale AFB, California/Taif	Aug/Mar
	Det 3	TR-1A/U-2R	RAF Akrotiri	Aug/Mar
17th RW	95th RS	TR-1A	RAF Alconbury/Taif	Aug/Mar
55th SRW	343rd SRS	RC-135U/V/W	Offutt AFB, Nevada/Riyadh Int'l Ap't	Aug/Mar
2nd BW	62nd & 596th BS	B-52G	Barksdale AFB, Louisiana/RAF Fairford	Feb/Mar
			Jeddah/King Abdul Aziz Int'l Ap't	Jan/Mar
42nd BW	69th BS	B-52G	Loring AFB, Maine/Diego Garcia	Aug/Mar
			Jeddah/King Abdul Aziz Int'l Ap't	Jan/Mar
93rd BW	328th BTS	B-52G	Castle AFB, California/Diego Garcia	Aug
			Jeddah/King Abdul Aziz Int'l Ap't	Jan/Mar
			RAF Fairford	Feb/Mar
97th BW	340th BS	B-52G	Eaker AFB, Arizona/Diego Garcia	Jan/Mar
379th BW	524th BS	B-52G	Wurtsmith AFB, Michigan/Jeddah/King	
			Abdul Aziz Int'l Ap't	Jan/Mar
			RAF Fairford	Feb/Mar
			Moron AB	Feb
416th BW	668th BS	B-52G	Griffiss AFB, New York/Jeddah/King	
			Abdul Aziz Int'l Ap't	Jan/Mar
			RAF Fairford	Feb/Mar
			Moron AB	Feb/Mar

Strategic Air Command (inflight-refuelling tankers)

2nd BW	32nd ARS	KC-10A	Barksdale AFB, Louisiana/Milan-Malpensa Ap't & Zaragoza AB	Jan/Mar
	71st ARS	KC-135A	Barksdale AFB, Louisiana/unrevealed	
5th BW	906th ARS	KC-135A	Minot AFB, North Dakota/unrevealed	
7th BW	7th ARS	KC-135A	Carswell AFB, Texas/unrevealed	
9th SRW	349th & 350th ARS	KC-135Q	Beale AFB, California/Riyadh	Aug/Mar
19th ARW	99th & 912th ARS	KC-135R	Robins AFB, Georgia/Mont-de-Marsan AB France	Feb/ Mar
			Muscat-Seeb	Aug
			Riyadh/King Khalid Int'l Ap't	Jan
22nd ARW	6th & 9th ARS	KC-10A	March AFB, California/Jeddah/King Abdul Aziz Int'l Ap't	Jan/Mar
28th BW	28th ARS	KC-135R	Ellsworth AFB, South Dakota/Al Dhafra	Aug
			Muscat-Seeb	Aug
42nd BW	42nd & 407th ARS	KC-135R	Loring AFB, Maine/unrevealed	Feb
68th ARW	344th & 911th ARS	KC-10A	Seymour Johnson AFB, North Carolina/Jeddah/King Abdul Aziz Int'l Ap't	Jan/Mar
92nd BW	43rd & 92nd ARS	KC-135A/R	Fairchild AFB, Washington/unrevealed	
93rd BW	93rd & 924th ARS	KC-135A/R	Castle AFB, California/unrevealed	
96th BW	917th ARS	KC-135A	Dyess AFB, Texas/unrevealed	Aug
			Incirlik AB	Jan/Mar
97th BW	97th ARS	KC-135A	Eaker AFB, Arizona/Jeddah/King Abdul Aziz Int'l Ap't	
301st ARW	? ARS	KC-135R	Malmstrom AFB, Montana/Masirah	Dec
			Muscat-Seeb	Aug
305th ARW	70th & 305th ARS	KC-135R	Grissom AFB, Indiana/Al Dhafra	Sep
			Riyadh/King Khalid Int'l Ap't	Jan
		EC-135L	Riyadh/King Khalid Int'l Ap't	Jan/Mar
319th BW	905th ARS	KC-135R	Grand Forks AFB, North Dakota/Al Dhafra	Aug
			Muscat-Seeb	Aug
			Riyadh/King Khalid Int'l Ap't	
340th ARW	11th & 306th ARS	KC-135R	Altus AFB, Oklahoma/Al Dhafra	
376th SW	909th ARS	KC-135A	Kadena AB/Riyadh/King Khalid Int'l Ap't	Jan
379th BW	920th ARS	KC-135A	Wurtsmith AFB, Michigan/unrevealed	Aug
380th BW	310th & 380th ARS	KC-135A/Q	Plattsburgh AFB, New York/Riyadh/King Khalid Int'l Ap't	Oct/ Mar
384th ARW	384th ARS	KC-135R	McConnell AFB, Kansas/Al Dhafra	Aug
			Masirah	Dec
410th BW	46th & 307th ARS	KC-135A	K. I. Sawyer AFB, Michigan/unrevealed	Aug
416th BW	41st ARS	KC-135R	Griffiss AFB, New York/Al Dhafra	Aug

Pacific Air Forces

3rd TFW	3rd TFS	F-4E	Clark AB/Incirlik AB	

Tactical Air Command

1st TFW	27th & 71st TFS	F-15C/D	Langley AFB, Virginia/Dhahran Int'l Ap't	Aug/Mar
4th TFW	335th TFS	F-15E	Seymour Johnson AFB, North Carolina/Al Kharj	Dec/Mar
	336th TFS	F-15E	Seymour Johnson AFB, North Carolina/Thumrait & Al Kharj	Aug & Jan/Mar
23rd TFW	74th &76th TFS	A-10A	England AFB, Louisiana/Damman/King Fahd Ap't	Aug/Mar
33rd TFW	58th TFS	F-15C/D	Eglin AFB, Florida/Tabuk/King Faisal AB	Sep/Mar
35th TFW	561st TFS	F-4G	George AFB, California/Sheikh Isa	Aug/Mar
37th TFW	415th & 416th TFS	F-117A	Tonopah TR, Nevada/ Khamis Mushait AB	Aug/Mar
67th TRW	12th TRS	RF-4C	Bergstrom AFB, Texas/Sheikh Isa	Jan/Mar
347th TFW	69th TFS	F-16C/D	Moody AFB, Georgia/Al Minhad	Jan/Mar
354th TFW	353rd & 355th TFS	A-10A	Myrtle Beach AFB, South Carolina/Damman/King Fahd Ap't	Aug/Mar
363rd TFW	17th & 33rd TFS	F-16C/D	Shaw AFB, South Carolina/Al Dhafra	Aug/Mar
366th TFW	390th ECS	EF-111A	Mountain Home AFB, Idaho/Taif	Aug/Mar

Wing	Squadron	Aircraft	Base/Deployment	Dates
388th TFW	4th & 421st TFS	F-16C/D	Hill AFB, Utah/Al Minhad	Jan/Mar
507th TACW	none	none	Shaw AFB, South Carolina/ Riyadh	Aug/Mar
552nd AW&CW				
963rd, 964th & 965th AW&CS		E-3B/C	Tinker AFB, Oklahoma/Riyadh/ Military City Ap't	Aug/Mar
	7th ACCS	EC-130E	Keesler AFB, Mississippi/Riyadh/Military City Ap't	Jan/Mar
	41st ECS	EC-130H	Davis Monthan AFB, Arizona/Riyadh/Military City Ap't	Jan/Mar
602nd TACW	23rd TASS	OA-10A	Davis Monthan AFB, Arizona/Damman/King Fahd Ap't	Nov/Mar

United States Air Forces in Europe

Wing	Squadron	Aircraft	Base/Deployment	Dates
10th TFW	511th TFS	A-10A	RAF Alconbury/Damman/King Fahd Ap't	Dec/Mar
20th TFW	79th TFS	F-111E	RAF Upper Heyford/Incirlik AB	Aug/Mar
(55th & 77th TFSs also rotated to Incirlik, but 79th TFS was main unit)				
26th TRW	38th TRS	RF-4C	Zweibrücken AB/Incirlik AB	Mar
36th TFW	53rd TFS	F-15C/D	Bitburg AB/Al Kharj	Jan/Mar
	525th TFS	F-15C/D	Bitburg AB/Incirlik AB	Dec/Mar
48th TFW	492nd, 493rd & 494th TFS	F-111F	RAF Lakenheath/Taif	Aug/Mar
50th TFW	10th TFS	F-16C/D	Hahn AB/Al Dhafra	Nov/Mar
52nd TFW	23rd TFS	F-4G & F-16C/D	Spangdahlem AB/Incirlik AB	Jan/Mar
	81st TFS	F-4G	Spangdahlem AB/Sheikh Isa	Sep/Mar
66th ECW	42nd ECS	EF-111A	RAF Upper Heyford/Incirlik AB	Dec/Mar
	43rd ECS	EC-130H	Sembach AB/Incirlik AB	Jan/Mar
401st TFW	612th TFS	F-16C/D	Torrejon AB/Incirlik AB	Jan/Mar
	614th TFS	F-16C/D	Torrejon AB/Doha	Aug/Mar
32nd TFG	32nd TFS	F-15C/D	Soesterberg AB	Jan/Mar

Air Force Reserve

Wing	Squadron	Aircraft	Base/Deployment	Dates
403rd TAW	815th TAS	C-130H	Keesler AFB, Mississippi/unrevealed	
434th ARW	72nd ARS	KC-135E	Grissom AFB, Indiana/Jeddah/King Abdul Aziz Int'l Ap't	Aug/Mar
452nd ARW	336th ARS	KC-135E	March AFB, California/Jeddah/KingAbdul Aziz Int'l Ap't	Aug/Mar
907th TAG	356th TAS	C-130E	Rickenbacker ANGB, Ohio	Oct/Mar
913th TAG	327th TAS	C-130E	NAS Willow Grove, Pennsylvania/Thumrait	
9145h TAG	328th TAS	C-130E	Niagara Falls IAP, New York/Sharjah	
926th TFG	706th TFS	A-10A	NAS New Orleans, Louisiana/ Al Damman/ King Fahd Ap't	Dec/Mar
927th TAG	63rd TAS	C-130E	Selfridge ANGB/Mississippi/Sharjah	Oct/Mar
939th ARW	71st SOS	HH-3E	Davis Monthan AFB, Arizona/unrevealed	
940th ARG	314th ARS	KC-135E	Mather AFB, California/Jeddah/King Abdul Aziz Int'l Ap't	

Air National Guard

Wing	Squadron	Aircraft	Base/Deployment	Dates
117th TRW	106th TRS	RF-4C	Birmingham MAP, Alabama/Sheikh Isa	Aug/Mar
126th ARW	108th ARS	KC-135E	Chicago-O'Hare IAP, Illinois/Jeddah/ King Abdul Aziz Int'l Ap't	Sep/Mar
141st ARW	116th ARS	KC-135E	Fairchild AFB, Washington/Cairo West	
190th ARG	117th ARS	KC-135E	Forbes Field, Kansas/Jeddah/King Abdul Aziz Int'l Ap't	Aug/Mar
128th ARG	126th ARS	KC-135E	General Mitchell IAP, Wisconsin/Cairo West	Sep
130th TAG	130th TAS	C-130H	Yeager Airport Charleston, West Virginia/Al Ain/Damman/ King Fahd Ap't	Oct/Mar
101st ARW	132nd ARS	KC-135E	Bangor IAP, Maine/Jeddah/King Abdul Aziz Int'l Ap't	
157th ARG	133rd ARS	KC-135E	Pease AFB, New Hampshire/Jeddah/King Abdul Aziz Int'l Ap't	
174th TFW	138th TFS	F-16A/B	Hancock Field Syracuse, New York/Al Kharj	Dec/Mar
166th TAG	142nd TAS	C-130H	Gtr Wilmington Ap't, Delaware/Al Ain/Al Kharj	Oct/Mar
160th ARG	145th ARS	KC-135E	Rickenbacker ANGB, Ohio/Jeddah/King Abdul Aziz Int'l Ap't	Jan/Mar
			Dubai Int'l Ap't	Feb/Mar
171st ARW	147th ARS	KC-135E	Gtr Pittsburgh IAP, Pennsylvania/Jeddah/King Abdul Aziz Int'l Ap't	Jan/Mar
			Dubai Int'l Ap't	Jan/Mar
170th ARG	150th ARS	KC-135E	McGuire ANGB, New Jersey/unrevealed	Sep
134th ARG	151st ARS	KC-135E	McGhee Tyson Ap't Knoxville, Tennessee/Jeddah/King Abdul Aziz Int'l Ap't	Aug/Mar
			Dubai Int'l Ap't	Feb/Mar
169th TFG	157th TFS	F-16A/B	McEntire ANGB, South Carolina/Al Kharj	Dec/Mar
168th ARG	168th ARS	KC-135E	Eielson AFB, Alaska/Jeddah/King Abdul Aziz Int'l Ap't	Aug/Mar
139th TAG	180th TAS	C-130H	Rosecrans MAP, Missouri/Al Ain	Sep/Mar
136th TAW	181st ARS	KC-135E	NAS Dallas, Texas/Al Ain/Damman/King Fahd Ap't	Sep/Mar
151st ARG	191st ARS	KC-135E	Salt Lake City IAP, Utah/Jeddah/ King Abdul Aziz Int'l Ap't	Aug/Mar
152nd TRG	192nd TRS	RF-4C	Reno-Cannon IAP, Nevada/Sheikh Isa	Dec/Mar
193rd SOG	193rd SOS	EC-130E	Harrisburgh IAP, Pennsylvania/ Riyadh/Mil City Ap't & Bateen	Aug/Mar
161st ARG	197th ARS	KC-135E	Phoenix/Sky Harbor IAP, Arizona/unrevealed	Sep

US NAVY

Air-capable ships involved in 'Desert Storm' between 17 January and 28 February 1991

USS *Midway* (CV-41) with 'NF ' tail code (sailed 2 October)

CVW-5	VFA-151	F/A-18A
	VFA-192	F/A-18A
	VFA-195	F/A-18A
	VA-115	A-6E
	VA-185	A-6E/KA-6D
	VAW-115	E-2C
	VAQ-136	EA-6B
	HS-12	SH-3H

USS *Saratoga* (CV-60) with 'AA' tail code (sailed 7 August)

CVW-17	VF-74	F-14A (Plus)
	VF-103	F-14A (Plus)
	VFA-81	F/A-18C
	VFA-83	F/A-18C
	VA-35	A-6E/KA-6D
	VAW-125	E-2C
	VAQ-132	EA-6B
	VS-30	S-3B
	HS-3	SH-3H

USS *Ranger* (CV-61) with 'NE' tail code (sailed 8 December)

CVW-2	VF-1	F-14A
	VF-2	F-14A
	VA-145	A-6E/KA-6D
	VA-155	A-6E
	VAW-116	E-2C
	VAQ-131	EA-6B
	VS-38	S-3A
	HS-14	SH-3H

USS *America* (CV-66) with 'AB' tail code (sailed 28 December)

CVW-1	VF-33	F-14A
	VF-102	F-14A
	VFA-82	F/A-18C
	VFA-86	F/A-18C
	VA-85	A-6E/KA-6D
	VAW-123	E-2C
	VAQ-137	EA-6B
	VS-32	S-3B
	HS-11	SH-3H

USS *John F. Kennedy* (CV-67) with 'AC' tail code (sailed 15 August)

CVW-3	VF-14	F-14A
	VF-32	F-14A
	VA-46	A-7E
	VA-72	A-7E
	VA-75	A-6E/KA-6D
	VAW-126	E-2C
	VAQ-130	EA-6B
	VS-22	S-3B
	HS-7	SH-3H

USS *Theodore Roosevelt* (CVN-71) with tail code 'AJ' (sailed 28 December)

CVW-8	VF-41	F-14A
	VF-84	F-14A
	VFA-15	F/A-18A

VFA-87	F/A-18A
VA-36	A-6E
VA-65	A-6E/KA-6D
VAW-124	E-2C
VAQ-141	EA-6B
VS-24	S-3A
HS-9	SH-3H

SQUADRON EQUIPMENT AND CARRIER AIR WING ASSIGNMENTS

Unit	Aircraft type	Carrier air wing	Home base
VF-1	F-14A	CVW-2	NAS Miramar, California
VF-2	F-14A	CVW-2	NAS Miramar, California
VF-14	F-14A	CVW-3	NAS Oceana, Virginia
VF-32	F-14A	CVW-3	NAS Oceana, Virginia
VF-33	F-14A	CVW-1	NAS Oceana, Virginia
VF-41	F-14A	CVW-8	NAS Oceana, Virginia
VF-74	F-14A (Plus)	CVW-17	NAS Oceana, Virginia
VF-84	F-14A	CVW-8	NAS Oceana, Virginia
VF-102	F-14A	CVW-1	NAS Oceana, Virginia
VF-103	F-14A (Plus)	CVW-17	NAS Oceana, Virginia
VA-46	A-7E	CVW-3	NAS Cecil Field, Florida
VA-72	A-7E	CVW-3	NAS Cecil Field, Florida
VFA-15	F/A-18A	CVW-8	NAS Cecil Field, Florida
VFA-81	F/A-18C	CVW-17	NAS Cecil Field, Florida
VFA-82	F/A-18C	CVW-1	NAS Cecil Field, Florida
VFA-83	F/A-18C	CVW-17	NAS Cecil Field, Florida
VFA-86	F/A-18C	CVW-1	NAS Cecil Field. Florida
VFA-87	F/A-18A	CVW-8	NAS Cecil Field, Florida
VFA-151	F/A-18A	CVW-5	NAS Atsugi, Japan
VFA-192	F/A-18A	CVW-5	NAS Atsugi, Japan
VFA-195	F/A-18A	CVW-5	NAS Atsugi, Japan
VA-35	A-6E/KA-6D	CVW-17	NAS Oceana, Virginia
VA-36	A-6E	CVW-8	NAS Oceana, Virginia
VA-65	A-6E/KA-6D	CVW-8	NAS Oceana, Virginia
VA-75	A-6E/KA-6D	CVW-3	NAS Oceana, Virginia
VA-85	A-6E/KA-6D	CVW-1	NAS Oceana, Virginia
VA-115	A-6E	CVW-5	NAS Atsugi, Japan
VA-145	A-6E/KA-6D	CVW-2	NAS Whidbey Island, Washington
VA-155	A-6E	CVW-2	NAS Whidbey Island, Washington
VA-185	A-6E/KA-6D	CVW-5	NAS Atsugi, Japan
VAW-115	E-2C	CVW-5	NAS Atsugi, Japan
VAW-116	E-2C	CVW-2	NAS Miramar, California
VAW-123	E-2C	CVW-1	NAS Norfolk, Virginia
VAW-124	E-2C	CVW-8	NAS Norfolk, Virginia
VAW-125	E-2C	CVW-17	NAS Norfolk, Virginia
VAW-126	E-2C	CVW-3	NAS Norfolk, Virginia
VAQ-130	EA-6B	CVW-3	NAS Whidbey Island, Washington
VAQ-131	EA-6B	CVW-2	NAS Whidbey Island, Washington
VAQ-132	EA-6B	CVW-17	NAS Whidbey Island, Washington
VAQ-136	EA-6B	CVW-5	NAS Atsugi, Japan
VAQ-137	EA-6B	CVW-1	NAS Whidbey Island, Washington
VAQ-141	EA-6B	CVW-8	NAS Whidbey Island, Washington
VS-22	S-3B	CVW-3	NAS Cecil Field, Florida
VS-24	S-3A	CVW-8	NAS Cecil Field, Florida
VS-30	S-3B	CVW-17	NAS Cecil Field, Florida
VS-32	S-3B	CVW-1	NAS Cecil Field, Florida
VS-38	S-3A	CVW-2	NAS North Island, California
HS-3	SH-3H	CVW-17	NAS Jacksonville, Florida
HS-7	SH-3H	CVW-3	NAS Jacksonville, Florida
HS-9	SH-3H	CVW-8	NAS Jacksonville, Florida
HS-11	SH-3H	CVW-1	NAS Jacksonville, Florida
HS-12	SH-3H	CVW-5	NAS Atsugi, Japan
HS-14	SH-3H	CVW-2	NAS North Island, California

US MARINE CORPS

Unit	Aircraft type	Forward base/home base	Dates in theatre
3rd Marine Air Wing (1st Marine Expeditionary Force)			
MAG-11			
VMFA(AW)-121	F/A-18D	Sheikh Isa/MCAS El Toro, California	Jan/Mar
VMFA-212	F/A-18C	Sheikh Isa/MCAS Kaneohe Bay, Hawaii	Dec/Mar
VMFA-232	F/A-18C	Sheikh Isa/MCAS Kaneohe Bay, Hawaii	Dec/Mar
VMFA-235	F/A-18C	Sheikh Isa/MCAS Kaneohe Bay, Hawaii	Aug/Mar
VMFA-314	F/A-18A	Sheikh Isa/MCAS Beaufort, South Carolina	Aug/Mar
VMFA-333	F/A-18A	Sheikh Isa/MCAS Beaufort, South Carolina	Aug/Mar
VMFA-451	F/A-18A	Sheikh Isa/MCAS Beaufort, South Carolina	Aug/Mar
VMA(AW)-224	A-6E	Sheikh Isa/MCAS Cherry Point, North Carolina	Aug/Mar
VMA(AW)-533	A-6E	Sheikh Isa/MCAS Cherry Point, North Carolina	Dec/Mar
VMAQ-2	EA-6B	Sheikh Isa/MCAS Cherry Point, North Carolina	Aug/Mar
VMGR-234	KC-130T	Bahrain/NAS Glenview, Illinois	Sep/Mar
VMGR-252	KC-130F/R	Bahrain/MCAS Cherry Point, North Carolina	Nov/Mar
VMGR-352	KC-130F/R	Bahrain/MCAS El Toro, California	Nov/Mar
VMGR-452	KC-130T	Bahrain, Al Jubail & Sheikh Isa/Stewart ANGB, New York	Sep/Mar
MCAS El Toro	UC-12B	Bahrain/MCAS El Toro, California	Aug/Mar
MCAS Yuma	UC-12B	Bahrain/MCAS Yuma, Arizona	Feb/Mar
MAG-13			
VMA-231	AV-8B	Al Jubail/MCAS Cherry Point, North Carolina	Dec/Mar
VMA-311	AV-8B	Al Jubail/MCAS Yuma, Arizona	Dec/Mar
VMA-542	AV-8B	Al Jubail/MCAS Cherry Point, North Carolina	Dec/Mar
VMA-513 Det B	AV-8B	Al Jubail/MCAS Yuma, Arizona	Dec/Mar
VMO-1	OV-10A/D	Al Jubail/MCAS New River, North Carolina	Sep/Mar
VMO-2	OV-10A/D	Al Jubail/MCAS Camp Pendleton, California	Sep/Mar

(The AV-8B force initially deployed to Sheikh Isa in August and September 1990, but moved to Abdul Aziz in December when the facility was upgraded to accept operations by STOVL aircraft. The AV-8B aircraft later operated from a number of forward positions including Kabrit and Tanajib.)

Unit	Aircraft type	Forward base/home base	Dates in theatre
MAG-16			
HMM-161	CH-46E	Abdul Aziz/MCAS Tustin, California	Nov/Mar
HMM-165	CH-46E	unrevealed/MCAS Kaneohe Bay, Hawaii	
HMLA-367	AH-1W &		
	UH-1N	Abdul Aziz/MCAS Futenma, Okinawa	Sep/Mar
HMLA-369	AH-1W &		
	UH-1N	Abdul Aziz/MCAS Camp Pendleton, California	Sep/Mar
HMH-462	CH-53D	Abdul Aziz/MCAS Tustin, California	Nov/Mar
HMH-463	CH-53D	Abdul Aziz/MCAS Kaneohe Bay, Hawaii	
HMH-465	CH-53E	Abdul Aziz & Ras al Gar/MCAS Tustin, California	Feb/Mar
HMH-466	CH-53E	Ras al Gar/MCAS Tustin, California	Feb/Mar
MAG-26			
HMM-261	CH-46E	Abdul Aziz/MCAS New River, North Carolina	
HMM-266	CH-46E	Abdul Aziz/MCAS New River, North Carolina	
HMM-774	CH-46E	unrevealed/NAS Norfolk, Virginia	Dec/Mar
HMH-362	CH-53D	unrevealed/MCAS New River, North Carolina	
HMH-464	CH-53E	Ras al Gar/MCAS New River, North Carolina	Feb/Mar
HMH-772	RH-53D	Abdul Aziz/NAS Alameda, California	Dec/Mar
HMA-775	AH-1J	Abdul Aziz/MCAS Camp Pendleton, California	Dec/Mar
HML-767	UH-1N	Abdul Aziz/NAS New Orleans, Louisiana	Dec/Mar
4th Marine Expeditionary Brigade			
MAG-40			
VMA-331	AV-8B	USS Nassau/MCAS Cherry Point, North Carolina	Nov/Mar
HMM-263	CH-46E	various ships/MCAS New River, North California	
HMM-365	CH-46E	various ships/MCAS New River, North Carolina	
HMH-461	CH-53E	various ships/MCAS New River, North Carolina	
HMLA-269	AH-1W &		
	UH-1N	various ships & Dhahran/MCAS New River, North Carolina	

5th Marine Expeditionary Brigade

MAG-50

HMM-265	CH-46E	USS *Tarawa* & USS *New Orleans*/MCAS Kaneohe Bay, Hawaii	
HMM-268	CH-46E	USS *Tarawa* & USS *New Orleans*/MCAS Tustin, California	
HMH-466 Det	CH-53E	USS *Tarawa* & USS *New Orleans*/MCAS Tustin, California	Nov
HMLA-169	AH-1W &		
	UH-1N	USS *Tarawa* & USS *New Orleans*/MCAS Camp Pendleton, California	Jan/Mar
HMA-773	AH-1J	USS *Tarawa* & USS *New Orleans*/NAS Atlanta, Georgia	Jan/Mar

13th Marine Expeditionary Unit

HMM-164	CH-46E	USS *Okinawa*/MCAS Tustin, California

US ARMY

Formation or unit	Aircraft types	Home base	Dates in theatre
82nd Airborne Division	OH-58A/D, UH-60A, AH-64A	Fort Bragg, North Carolina	Aug/Mar
101st Airborne Division	CH-47D, OH-58A/D,		
	UH-60A & AH-64A	Fort Rucker, Alabama	Aug/Mar
501st Bat/1st Armored Div	UH-1H, UH-60A & AH-64A		Jan/Mar
502nd Bat/2nd Armored Div	UH-1H & AH-64A		Jan/Mar
503rd Bat/3rd Armored Div	UH-1H, UH-60A & AH-1S		Jan/Mar
1st Bat/1st Aviation Reg	UH-1H	Ansbach, Germany	Jan/Mar
2nd Bat/1st Aviation Reg	OH-58C, UH-60A & AH-64A	Ansbach, Germany	Jan/Mar
3rd Bat/1st Aviation Reg	OH-58C, UH-60A & AH-64A	Ansbach, Germany	Jan/Mar
5th Bat/158th Aviation Reg	OH-58D	Bonames, Germany	Jan/Mar
6th Bat/158th Aviation Reg	UH-60A	Wiesbaden, Germany	Jan/Mar
4th Bat/159th Aviation Reg	UH-1H & OH-58D	Stuttgart, Germany	Jan/Mar
5th Bat/159th Aviation Reg	UH-1H & CH-47D	Schwabisch-Hall, Germany	Jan/Mar
6th Bat/159th Aviation Reg	UH-1H, CH-47D & UH-60A	Schwabisch-Hall, Germany	Jan/Mar
7th Bat/159th Aviation Reg	UH-1H & CH-47D	Nellingen, Germany	Jan/Mar
2nd Bat/227th Aviation Reg	AH-64A	Hanau, Germany	Jan/Mar
3rd Bat/227th Aviation Reg	AH-64A	Hanau, Germany	Jan/Mar
2nd Bat/229th Aviation Reg	AH-64A	Illesheim, Germany	Jan/Mar
4th Bat/229th Aviation Reg	OH-58C, UH-60A & AH-64A	Illesheim, Germany	Jan/Mar
2nd Bat/?th Cavalry Reg	OH-58C, UH-60A & AH-64A	Illesheim, Germany	Jan/Mar
3rd Bat/?th Cavalry Reg	OH-58C, UH-60A & AH-64A	Wiesbaden, Germany	Jan/Mar
5th Bat/?th Cavalry Reg	AH-64A	Wiesbaden, Germany	Jan/Mar
70th Transport Bat	UH-1H		Jan/Mar
Task Force Phoenix	OH-58D, UH-60A & EH-60C	Bad Kreuznach & Mainz-Finthen,	
		Germany	Jan/Mar
Task Force Skyhawk	OH-58D	Ansbach, Germany	Jan/Mar
Task Force Viper	OH-58C & EH-60C	Hanau, Germany	Jan/Mar
1st Cavalry Division	UH-1H & AH-64A		Jan/Mar
6th Cavalry Division	OH-58C, UH-60A & AH-64A		Jan/Mar
1st Infantry Division	UH-1H, AH-1S & UH-60A		Jan/Mar
24th Infantry Division	UH-1H, AH-1S & UH-60A		Jan/Mar
236th Medical Company	UH-60A	Landstuhl, Germany	Jan/Mar
1st Mil Intel Bat	RC-12D	Wiesbaden, Germany	Jan/Mar
2nd Mil Intel Bat	RC-12D & OV/RV-1D	Stuttgart, Germany	Jan/Mar
224th Mil Intel Bat	RU-21H & OV/RV-1D		Sep

US AIRCRAFT PROVISIONAL TOTAL FOR OPERATION 'DESERT STORM' (EXCLUDING ASSETS IN TURKEY): 3,614

US Air Force	US Navy	US Marine Corps	US Army
F-16 (210)	F/A-18 (89)	F/A-18 (78)	AH-64 (237)
F-15 (96)	A-6E (95)	A-6E (2)	AH-1 (131)
F-15E (48)	A-7E (24)	EA-6B (12)	UH-60 (299)
F-4G (48)	F-14 (92)	AV-8B (6)	UH-60V (64)
F-117 (42)	F-14/TARPS (14)	OV-10 (13)	EH-60 (24)

F-111 (64)	EA-6B (27)	KC-130 (15)	OH-58C (295)
EF-111A (18)	E-2C (29)	AH-1 (40)	OH-58D (92)
B-52 (86)	S-3 (48)	CH-53 (40)	UH-1 (193)
KC-135 (194)	P-3 (?)	CH-46 (6)	UH-1V (121)
EC-135L (2)	EP-3E (?)	UH-1 (30)	CH-47 (127)
KC-10 (30)			MH-47 (4)
A-10A (194)			
C-130 (132)			
E-3 (11)			
E-8 (2)			
RF-4C (18)			
EC-130 (9)			
HC-130 (4)			
MC-130 (4)			
AC-130 (4)			
HH-3/MH-53 (22)			
1,238	421	368	1,587

to which should be added non-quantifiable numbers of the following types: C-21, EA-3B, RC-12, RC-135, SH-3H, C-12, U-2T & TR-1, C-23, RV/OV-1, RU-21 and AH/MH-6

Non-American Coalition Forces

UNITED KINGDOM (OPERATION 'GRANBY')

Support Helicopter Force Middle East/Army Air Corps

Helicopter type	Provenance
Chinook HC 1	No. 7 Sqn lead with No. 18 Sqn & No. 240 OCU (RAF Gütersloh & Odiham)
Puma HC 1	No. 230 Sqn lead with No. 33 Sqn (RAF Gütersloh & Odiham)
Sea King HAS 5	C Flt No. 826 Sqn (embarked on RFA Olna & RFA Sir Galahad as well as other ships)
Sea King HC 4	Nos 845, 848 & 846 Sqns (last embarked on RFA Fort Grange & Argus)
Lynx HAS 3GM	No. 815 Sqn (embarked on HMS Cardiff, Gloucester, London & Manchester) and No. 829 Sqn (embarked on HMS Brazen)

Unit	Helicopter types (supporting British 1st Armoured Division)
No. 654 Sqn	Gazelle AH 1 & Lynx AH 7
No. 659 Sqn	Gazelle AH 1 & Lynx AH 7
No. 661 Sqn	Gazelle AH 1 & Lynx AH 7

Royal Air Force

Unit	Aircraft type	Provenance
DHAHRAN		
Tornado Det	Tornado GR 1 & 1A	No. 31 Sqn lead with elements of Nos 2, 9, 13, 14 & 17 Sqns (RAF Brüggen, Honington, Laarbruch & Marham)
Tornado ADV Det	Tornado F 3	No. 43 Sqn lead with No. 29 Sqn (RAF Leuchars & Coningsby)
MUHARRAQ		
Buccaneer Det	Buccaneer S 2B	No. 208 Sqn lead with No. 12 Sqn & No. 237 OCU (RAF Lossiemouth)
Jaguar Det	Jaguar GR 1A	No. 41 Sqn lead with elements of Nos 6 & 54 Sqns (RAF Coltishall)
Tornado Det	Tornado GR 1	No. 15 Sqn lead with elements of Nos 9, 17, 27, 31 & 617 Sqns (RAF Brüggen, Laarbruch & Marham)
Victor Det	Victor K 2	No. 55 Sqn (RAF Marham)
RIYADH/KING KHALID INTERNATIONAL AIRPORT		
RAF Air Transport Det	Hercules C 1P/3P	No. 242 OCU lead with elements of Nos 24, 30, 47 & 70 Sqns (RAF Lyneham) and No. 40 Sqn RNZAF
	VC10 K 2/3	No. 101 Sqn (RAF Brize Norton)
	TriStar K 1	No. 216 Sqn (RAF Brize Norton)
	BAe 125 CC 2/3	No. 32 Sqn (RAF Northolt)

TABUK

Tornado Det	Tornado GR 1	No. 16 Sqn lead with elements of Nos 2, 9, 13, 14, 20 & 617 Sqns (RAF Brüggen, Honington, Laarbruch & Marham)

SEEB

Nimrod MR Det	Nimrod MR 2P	No. 120 Sqn lead with Nos 42 & 206 Sqns (RAF Kinloss & St Mawgan)

UNCONFIRMED LOCATION

Nimrod R Det	Nimrod R 1P	No. 51 Sqn (RAF Wyton)

AUSTRALIA

Unconfirmed location

No. 37 Sqn	C-130E	Richmond AB

BAHRAIN

Sheikh Isa

Fighter Squadron	F-5E
Fighter Squadron	F-16C/D

CANADA (OPERATION 'FRICTION')

DOHA

Unit	Aircraft type	Home base
No. 409 Squadron	CF-18A	CFB Soellingen, Germany
No. 437 Squadron	CC-137	CFB Trenton
No. 439 Squadron	CF-18	CFB Soellingen, Germany
No. 441 Squadron	CF-18A	CFB Cold Lake

at sea on board HMCS Athabascan and Protecteur

No. 423 Squadron	CH-124A	CFB Halifax and Shearwater

FRANCE (OPERATION 'DAGUET')

Unit	Aircraft type	Home base

RIYADH/KING KHALID INTERNATIONAL AIRPORT

ET 60	ET 3/60	DC-8F	Paris-Charles de Gaulle
ET 61	ET 1, 2 & 3/61	C.160F & C-130H-30	Orleans-Bricy
ET 64	ET 1/64	C.160NG	Evreux-Fauville
ET 65	ET 1/65	Nord 262 & Mystère	Villacoublay
ERV 93	ERV 1, 2 & 3/93	C-135FR	Avord, Istres-le Tubé & Mont-de-Marsan

King Khalid Military City (later Rafha, then As Salman in Iraq)

RHC 'Daguet' 1er & 3ème RHC	Gazelle & Puma	Phalsbourg & Etain-Rouvres

Al Absa

EC 5	EC 1, 2 & 3/5	Mirage 2000C	Orange-Caritat
EC 11	EC 1, 2 & 3/11	Jaguar A	Toul-Rosières
	EC 4/11	Jaguar A	Bordeaux-Mérignac
ER 33	ER 1, 2 & 3/33	Mirage F1CR	Strasbourg-Entzheim
EE 54	EE 1/54	C.160 GABRIEL	Evreux-Fauville
EH 67	EH 1/67	SA 330B Puma	Cazaux

Doha (Operation 'Meteil')

EC 12	EC 1, 2 & 3/12	Mirage F1C	Cambrai-Epinoy

ITALY (OPERATION 'LOCUSTA')

Unit	Aircraft type	Provenance

Al Dhafra (Maqatra)

6° Stormo		Tornado IDS	154° Gruppo (Ghedi)
36° Stormo	Tornado IDS		156° Gruppo (Gioia del Colle)
50° Stormo		Tornado IDS	155° Gruppo (Piacenza/San Damiano)

KUWAIT (EXILE AIR FORCE)

Dhahran

Nos 9 & 25 Sqns	A-4KU & TA-4KU
Nos 18 & 61 Sqns	Mirage F1CK & Gazelle

King Khalid Military City

not available	SA 330 Puma & AS 532C Cougar

NEW ZEALAND

Riyadh/King Khalid International Airport

No. 40 Squadron	C-130H	assigned to RAF Air Transport Detachment (Whenuapai)

QATAR

Doha

No. 7 Squadron	Mirage F1EDA

SAUDI ARABIA

Dhahran

No. 7 Sqn	Tornado IDS
No. 13 Sqn	F-15C/D
No. 21 Sqn	Hawk
No. 29 Sqn	Tornado ADV
No. 34 Sqn	Tornado ADV
No. 37 Sqn	Hawk
No. 42 Sqn	F-15C/D
No. 66 Sqn	Tornado IDS (forming)

Jeddah/King Abdul Aziz Airport

No. 4 Sqn	C-130E/H & KC-130H

Khamis Mushait

No. 6 Sqn	unknown
No. 15 Sqn	F-5E/F

Riyadh/Military City Airport

No. 16 Sqn	C-130E/H & KC-130H
No. 18 Sqn	E-3A & KE-3A

Tabuk

No. 17 Sqn	F-5E/F, RF-5E & F-5B

Taif

No. 3 Sqn	F-5E/F
No. 5 Sqn	F-15C/D
No. 10 Sqn	F-5E/F

Saudi Navy

? Sqn	AS 565SA Panther	Ras al Jubail

SOUTH KOREA

Al Ain

? Sqn	C-130H	Pusan (?)

UNITED ARAB EMIRATES

Al Dhafra (Maqatra), Abu Dhabi

? Squadron	Mirage 2000EAD

COLOUR PLATES

1
Panavia Tornado IDS interdictor, s/n 766, Royal Saudi Air Force
A machine of the Royal Saudi Air Force's Nos 7 or 66 Squadrons based at Dhahran Air Base in Saudi Arabia

2
General Dynamics F-16C Fighting Falcon, 4th Tactical Fighter Squadron, US Air Force
This air combat and multi-role fighter, serial number unknown, was from the 4th or 421st Tactical Fighter Squadron of the US Air Force's 388th Tactical Fighter Wing. Normally based at Hill Air Force Base, Utah, the slightly restyled 388th TFW (Provisional) when parent to the 69th TFS of the 347th TFS (Moody AFB, Georgia) was located at Al Minhad in the United Arab Emirates

3
Fairchild Republic A-10A Thunderbolt II anti-tank and close support aircraft, s/n 80-186 'Tiger 1', 23rd Tactical Fighter Wing, US Air Force
This was the aeroplane of the commander of the US Air Force's 23rd Tactical Fighter Wing. Normally based at England Air Force Base, Louisiana, the 23rd TFW was located at King Fahd Airport, Riyadh, throughout the whole 'Desert Shield' and 'Desert Storm' period

4
McDonnell Douglas F-15C Eagle, s/n 82-046, 27th Tactical Fighter Sqn, US Air Force
An air-superiority fighter of the 27th Tactical Fighter Squadron of the US Air Force's 1st Tactical Fighter Wing (27th and 71st TFSs). Normally based at Langley Air Force Base, Virginia, the 1st TFW was located at Dhahran International Airport in Saudi Arabia between August 1990 and March 1991

5
McDonnell Douglas F-15E Eagle, s/n 89-0489, 335 Tactical Fighter Squadron, US Air Force
The 335th Tactical Fighter Squadron was part of the 4th Tactical Fighter Wing (Provisional). Normally based at Seymour Johnson Air Force Base, North Carolina as part of the Tactical Air Command, the 4th TFW was located at Al Kharj Air Base in Saudi Arabia between December 1990 and March 1991

6
General Dynamics F-111F, s/n 70-2390 'Miss Liberty II', 494th Tactical Fighter Sqn, US Air Force
This F-111F interdictor was the aeroplane of the commanding officer of the US Air Force's 48th Tactical Fighter Wing and operated within that wing's 494th Tactical Fighter Squadron. Normally based at RAF Lakenheath in the UK, the 48th TFW was located at Taif in Saudi Arabia between August 1990 and March 1991

7
Lockheed F-117A Night Hawk, s/n 813 'Toxic Avenger', 415-416th Tactical Fighter Sqns, US Air Force
This 'stealth' attack aircraft was from the US Air Force's 37th Tactical Fighter Wing (415th and 416th Tactical Fighter Squadrons). Normally based at Tonopah in Nevada, the 37th TFW was located at Khamis Mushait Air Force Base in Saudi Arabia between August 1990 and March 1991

8
Boeing B-52G Stratofortress heavy bomber, s/n 58-0204, 379th Bomb Wing, US Air Force
The US Air Force's 379th Bomb Wing was based at Wurtsmith Air Force Base, Michigan. This aircraft operated from forward bases indicated by the colour of the bomb-shaped mission markers on the fuselage: black for missions from Moron in Spain, white for missions from RAF Fairford in England, and white for missions from Jeddah in Saudi Arabia

9
Sikorsky MH-53J 'Pave Low', s/n unknown, Special Operations Sqns, US Air Force
This special operations helicopter was one of the machines operated by the US Air Force in Saudi Arabia by the 55th Special Operations Squadron of the 1st Special Operations Wing and the 21st Special Operations Squadron of the 39th Special Operations Wing. The 1st and 39th SOWs were normally based at Hurlburt Field (within Eglin Air Force Base), Florida and RAF Woodbridge, England respectively. The 55th SOS operated from unrevealed bases in Saudi Arabia between November 1990 and March 1991, while the 21st SOS operated from Incirlik and Batman Air Bases in Turkey between January and March 1991

10
McDonnell Douglas F/A-18C Hornet, s/n 163508, VFA-81 'Sunliners' Sqn, US Navy
This dual-role fighter and attack aircraft was a machine of the US Navy's VFA-81 'Sunliners' squadron of the CVW-17 wing embarked on the aircraft carrier USS *Saratoga* (CV-60), which sailed for the theatre on 7 August 1990

11
Grumman F-14A Tomcat, VF-32 'Swordsmen' Sqn, US Navy
A carrierborne fleet defence and air superiority fighter, serial number unknown. The 'Swordsmen' squadron of the CVW-3 wing embarked on the aircraft carrier USS *John F. Kennedy* (CV-67), which sailed for the theatre on 15 August 1990

12
Grumman A-6E Intruder, s/n 155661, VA-35 'Black Panthers' Sqn, US Navy
The 'Black Panthers' Squadron of the CVW-17 wing embarked on the aircraft carrier USS *Saratoga* (CV-60), which sailed for the theatre on 7 August 1990

13
McDonnell Douglas AH-64A Apache, s/n unknown, US Army
An anti-tank helicopter of the 2nd Battalion, 229th Aviation Regiment, a US Army unit normally based at Illesheim in Germany. The US Army's combat aviation arms (including two battalions of AH-64 Apache anti-tank helicopters) provided the capacity for deep strikes at the enemy's rear areas

14
Panavia Tornado GR 1 interdictor, s/n ZA477 'MiG Eater', RAF
A machine of the Tornado force based at Tabuk Air Base in Saudi Arabia and comprising elements led by No 16 Squadron, RAF, but including parts of Nos 2, 9, 13, 14, 20 and 617 Squadrons normally based at RAF Brüggen and Laarbruch in Germany, and RAF Honington and Marham in the UK

15
Westland Lynx HAS 3, s/n XZ256, No 815 Sqn, Fleet Air Arm
This anti-submarine and utility helicopter was normally based at RNAS Portland in the UK. The squadron provided helicopters for destroyers' and frigates' flights, and XZ256 was allocated to HMS *Brazen*

16
SEPECAT Jaguar A, s/n 103, Armée de l'Air
This French attack aircraft was one of the aircraft operated by the 2ème Escadrille of the Armée de l'Air's Escadron de Chasse 2/11 'Vosges'. Normally based at Toul-Rosières, EC 5 was located at Al Ahsa Air Base in Saudi Arabia

COLOUR SECTION

1
Fascinated members of the crew of the updated battleship USS *New Jersey* watch as a BGM-109 Tomahawk cruise missile is fired from their ship. Launched from a variety of platforms, such missiles provided a very accurate means of attacking point targets deep in Iraq.

2
Visible on the forward fuselage of this Panavia Tornado GR 1 interdictor are the radome over the radar equipment, the dark surround of the muzzle port for the starboard 27 mm Mauser cannon, and the retracted inflight-refuelling probe.

3
The Iraqi air defences made extensive use of anti-aircraft artillery of various light and medium calibres firing a high proportion of tracer projectiles.

4
The greatest threat to the coalition land offensive was thought to be from the Iraqi army's large armoured force, which therefore received special attention from the fixed-and rotary-winged aircraft of the coalition air forces, as well as the coalition's own armoured fighting vehicles and anti-tank guided missile teams.

5
Seen here with two bombs extended below the pair of side-by-side weapons bays in the lower fuselage, this is the first Lockheed F-117A Night Hawk to arrive at Khamis Mushait Air Base in Saudi Arabia.

6
A tractor operated by a member of the flight deck crew manoeuvres a Vought A-7E Corsair II on board an aircraft carrier of the US Navy, which retired its last A-7 aircraft from first-line service soon after the end of hostilities with Iraq.

7
Carrying two drop tanks, two tip-mounted AIM-9 Sidewinder short-range AAMs and at least one AIM-120A AMRAAM medium-range AAM, this McDonnell Douglas F/A-18 Hornet dual-role fighter and attack aircraft has just caught the arrester wire as it lands back on its parent carrier after a mission over Iraq.

8
Men of the US Army's 101st Airborne Division load AGM-114A Hellfire anti-tank missiles on a hardpoint under the stub wing of one of the divisional air brigade's McDonnell Douglas AH-64A Apache anti-tank helicopters.

9
Maintenance of aircraft of all types was especially difficult in Saudi Arabia, where great heat was accompanied by vast quantities of sand and dust seemingly eager to insinuate themselves into any and all orifices where they could cause damage to moving parts. This is the propeller of a Lockheed C-130 Hercules tactical transport with its spinner removed.

10
Armourers work on some of the diverse weapons required for a typical mission launched from the deck of one of the US Navy's aircraft carriers.

11
Carrying two AGM-88A HARM anti-radar missiles as its only weapons, the F-4G 'Wild Weasel' was vital to the survival of attack packages of coalition

aircraft by detecting and destroying the radars on which the Iraqis largely relied for the detection of targets and the guidance of surface-to-air missiles.

12
Complete with the hardbacks that attach to the hardpoints on the aircraft's pylons, stores rest on their movement trolleys for installation on Vought A-7E Corsair II attack aircraft.

INDEX

References to illustrations are shown in **bold**. Colour Plates and Colour Section illustrations are prefixed 'pl.' and 'cs.', with page and caption locators in brackets.